—African-American Biographies—

PAUL ROBESON

Actor, Singer, Political Activist

Series Consultant:
Dr. Russell L. Adams, Chairman
Department of Afro-American Studies, Howard University

David K. Wright

Enslow Publishers, Inc.

40 Industrial Road   PO Box 38
Box 398   Aldershot
Berkeley Heights, NJ 07922   Hants GU12 6BP
USA   UK

http://www.enslow.com

Library of Congress Cataloging-in-Publication Data

Wright, David K.
    Paul Robeson : actor, singer, political activist / David K. Wright.
        p.   cm. — (African-American biographies)
    Includes bibliographical references (p. 121) and index.
    Summary: Examines the life and career of the African-American singer-
actor who spoke out against racism and injustice.
    ISBN 0-89490-944-4
    1. Robeson, Paul, 1898–1976—Juvenile literature. 2. Afro-Americans—
Biography—Juvenile literature. 3. Actors—United States—Biography—
Juvenile literature. 4. Singers—United States—Biography—Juvenile
literature. 5. Political activists—United States—Biography—Juvenile
literature. [1. Robeson, Paul, 1898-1976. 2. Actors and actresses.
3. Singers. 4. Afro-Americans—Biography.] I. Title. I. Series.
E185.97.R63W755   1998
791'.092—dc21
[B]   97-34194
                                                                                  CIP
                                                                                   AC
Printed in the United States of America

10 9 8 7 6 5 4 3 2

Every effort has been made to locate all copyright holders of material used in
this book. If any errors or omissions have occurred, corrections will be made in
future editions of this book.

Illustration Credits: Courtesy of the Library of Congress, p. 56;
Courtesy of the Westfield Historical Society, Westfield, New Jersey, pp.
14, 17; Harris and Ewing Photo, courtesy of the D.C. Public Library,
Washingtoniana Division, p. 100; Photographs and Prints Division,
Schomburg Center for Research in Black Culture, The New York Public
Library, Astor, Lenox and Tilden Foundations, p. 43; Prints and
Photographs Department, Moorland-Spingarn Research Center, Howard
University, p. 110; Special Collections and University Archives, Rutgers
University Libraries, pp. 22, 24, 27, 31, 69, 92; Wisconsin Center for Film
and Theater Research, pp. 4, 35, 39, 46, 50, 61, 66, 78, 82, 89, 104.

Cover Illustration: Wisconsin Center for Film and Theater Research.

CONTENTS

Paul Robeson

1

VIOLENCE IN PEEKSKILL

eekskill, New York, in 1949 was a working-class village some forty miles north of New York City. Situated on the east bank of the Hudson River, the town was the hub of a busy summer tourist trade. Middle-class New York City residents owned vacation homes atop the hills and in the valleys around Peekskill. Some of the people who lived year-round in Peekskill did not like the vacationers. The visitors seemed to have more money than the locals; they worked in the dangerous, corrupt big city; many were Jews or other non-Christians; and several were Socialist or Communist sympathizers.

So when it was announced that Paul Robeson, the

famous African-American actor, singer, and political activist, would give a concert in a Peekskill park, there was swift local reaction. The daily newspaper accused Robeson of aiding subversives—of helping people who want to overthrow the government—even though he had performed in Peekskill in the past. Veterans' groups, such as the American Legion, wrote letters to the paper, stating that the entertainer was unwelcome in Peekskill. Virtually everyone else, from local politicians to the chamber of commerce, joined the disapproval. How could one man cause such a reaction?

Paul Robeson was no ordinary man. Born poor in a small town in New Jersey, he became an All-American football player, a superior college student, and one of very few African Americans at the time to graduate from law school. Added to these accomplishments were years of experience as a dramatic actor and a deep singing voice that could move even the least emotional listener to the brink of tears. He knew hundreds of old and new songs by heart, he spoke several languages, and he was famous throughout the world. Why were the people of Peekskill so upset at the prospect of a visit by such a talented performer?

The entertainer was a civil-rights activist in an era when comparatively few spoke up for the rights of minorities. He talked frankly, frequently stating opinions in public that most African Americans dared not utter. And he was well traveled, having performed on several continents. Besides the fact that he was black in a largely white town, Robeson's numerous visits to and longtime familiarity with the Soviet Union angered many patriotic Peekskill people.[1]

Peekskill residents knew little or nothing of Soviet society. But they, like many other Americans in those years, were against anything that tilted toward socialism or communism. One Socialist couple, who lived in New York City and owned a summer cottage near Peekskill, received phone threats and were called names as they shopped and as they worked in their yard. Some of the estimated twenty-five hundred people walking toward the concert were hit with rocks thrown by mobs of men as police idly stood by. A cross was set afire on a nearby hill.

Robeson, riding in a friend's car, crouched on the floor to hide. The driver somehow got out of the line of cars headed for the concert, turned around, and returned to New York City. Arriving in Harlem, Robeson held a news conference. He said the Peekskill riot reminded him of "Hitlerite Germany" and asked federal authorities to look into the matter.[2] He also promised to return to Peekskill for a concert one week later. Wisely, Robeson refused the offer of protection from Bumpy Johnson, Harlem's most notorious gangster.

By the following week, everyone in Peekskill seemed to be against holding the concert. This time, eight thousand military veterans from all over New York State marched in protest in front of the Peekskill park. They yelled anti-black and anti-Semitic obscenities, telling union members and others, "You came in but you don't get out" of the park alive.[3] Robeson took the stage at 4:00 P.M., flanked by fifteen burly union members acting as bodyguards. While he sang, roving unionists discovered two Peekskill men with rifles hiding in the area.

Whenever Paul Robeson sang, people listened. Even among the uneasy concert audience, the sound was magic. Deep yet somehow light, able to run up and down the scale, his voice effortlessly reached and held low notes only imagined by most male vocalists. A star in motion pictures, Robeson was generally recognized by the public during the pretelevision era. Millions had become enchanted at one time or another with his voice—one of the great voices of the twentieth century. Only baseball and boxing could draw a crowd comparable in size to that of a Robeson concert. Many in the big audience that afternoon cared little or nothing for politics. They just wanted to hear Paul Robeson sing.

The concert ended and the crowd started home—or made the attempt. Once again, the visitors were attacked. Rocks and bottles were thrown, and a number of people were bloodied. Police stood by watching. The star of the show was covered with a blanket and whisked from the scene in a fast-moving car. He was luckier than an estimated one hundred fifty concertgoers who required medical attention.

A grand jury later blamed Robeson and his audience for the confrontation. The grand jury may have been influenced by Governor Thomas E. Dewey, who ordered an investigation by some of the same people who had failed to keep order during the riot. The governor wanted to know if the concert had been scheduled for the purpose of disturbing the peace and whether the event was a "Communist strategy to foment racial and religious hatred."[4]

Paul Robeson's fans were attacked as they left the 1949 concert in Peekskill, New York. Angry rioters protesting the concert smashed this car's windshield and flipped it over.

To understand all this, it helps to understand what America was like in 1949. President Harry S. Truman had only recently integrated the armed forces; African-American children were not allowed in many public schools; and major-league baseball—the national pastime—had permitted African-American players for only two years. Many white Americans were obsessed with the notion that African Americans were second-class citizens. Even those whites who did not necessarily dislike black people still generally ignored them. Paul Robeson, by virtue of his talent, physical size, and intelligence, was difficult to ignore.

Some people found Robeson especially frightening. Many white Americans believed Communists were trying to recruit African Americans who realized how unfairly they had always been treated in the United States. Though African Americans were much more concerned with justice than with revolution, Paul Robeson loomed large in the minds of people in Peekskill and elsewhere. Where had he come from, what had he accomplished, and where would events take him?

2

A New Jersey Boyhood

aul Leroy Robeson was born in Princeton, New Jersey, on April 9, 1898. His father, William Drew Robeson, had been born into slavery in the pre–Civil War South. His mother, Maria Louisa Bustill Robeson, had a more mixed and happier family history. Her roots could be traced back to African ancestry and to Delaware Indians and English Quakers. Many of Louisa Robeson's forebears were middle class. They were active in the antislavery movement, in medicine, and in the newspaper business.

Some assumed that Paul was influenced mainly by his mother and her side of the family. Actually, it was his humble, strong-willed father who pointed Paul down his road in life. "The glory of my boyhood years was my father. I loved him like no one in all the world," Paul later recalled.[1]

William Robeson had escaped from slavery on the Roberson plantation in North Carolina in 1860 at the age of fifteen. He made his way to Pennsylvania, working as a civilian laborer for the Union army. He saved his money and eventually was accepted as a ministerial student at Lincoln University, near Philadelphia. The all-black school not only prepared him for religious work but also was the place where he met his future wife. Maria Louisa Bustill was teaching school in Philadelphia. They married in 1878, and over the next several years they had seven children. Paul was the youngest.

At the time of Paul's birth, his brother William Jr. was almost seventeen, John was twelve, Benjamin was six, and Marian was going on four. Two other siblings had died in infancy. Paul's father, William Robeson, was fifty-three years old and had served for almost two decades as pastor at a Presbyterian church for African Americans in Princeton. However, his future with the church no longer looked promising. Because of a number of religious disagreements with some powerful church members, the Reverend Robeson was forced to resign his ministry in 1901. Paul was not yet three years of age. His father found work wherever he could, preaching occasionally in a number of different churches. But an incident more tragic than meager employment would soon strike the family.

Most homes at the time had a central, potbelly stove that glowed with warmth every day from late fall to spring. The Robeson house was no exception. To keep it pumping out heat, coal had to be added on a regular basis. One day, apparently while she was fueling the stove, a hot coal fell on Louisa's dress. She quickly became engulfed in flames. Paul's mother lingered in great pain for several days before dying. The year was 1904 and Paul was not quite six years old.

Paul remembered little of his mother, other than that she was nearly blind and often not well. He could recall only a coffin, a funeral, and many relatives in the house. "Others have told me of her remarkable intellect," he once wrote, adding that his mother was his father's "right hand in all his community work."[2]

After his wife's death, William Robeson sent Ben and Marian to boarding schools. In 1907, the Reverend Robeson found work in a small grocery store in Westfield, New Jersey, and lived with Paul above the store. Several things happened to make the loss of Louisa bearable. Kindly neighbors saw to it that the Robesons had more food than they could eat. The large North Carolina Robeson clan also sent food to them on a regular basis—plump hams, raw and roasted peanuts, bags of vegetables, and more. The Reverend

Robeson switched religious affiliation, moving from the Presbyterian to the African Methodist Episcopal (A.M.E.) church. He soon was the leader of a small church with a loyal congregation.

In Westfield, Paul played on the school basketball and baseball teams. Years later, one of his Westfield teammates recalled that Robeson was "a shy kid, who did everything well, but preferred to keep in the background." He added, "I never saw him lose his temper or show resentment. All the boys liked him."[3]

St. Luke's A.M.E. Zion Church, built in 1908 by William Robeson and his congregation, still stands today in Westfield, New Jersey.

Paul could recall disobeying his father only once in his life. He was ten years old and his father summoned him for failing to do as he was told. Instead of walking obediently toward his father, Paul ran across the street. Following after him, his father fell, knocking out a tooth. Seeing his father in pain for something he had done, Paul was overwhelmed with shame and grief. The incident made Paul feel that he had hurt the person he most loved in the whole world, a feeling that stayed with him for the rest of his days.[4]

Ben went off to study for the ministry, and Paul and his father became quite close. Paul walked to school, where he was a superior student. After school, he showed an interest in sports, playing football, running track, and shooting basketball. After finishing his homework in the evening, Paul would share his father's interest in speechmaking by memorizing and then reciting many of history's famous orations. Religion also played an important part in his early life. The Reverend Robeson taught Paul the difference between right and wrong, and he carried a strong sense of that into adulthood. Paul grew taller and stronger than most of his classmates and was remembered as an obedient, happy child. He believed that hard work, honesty, and reason were the answers to almost everything.

But all was not happiness in Somerville, New Jersey. Paul and his father had moved there in 1910, when the Reverend Robeson was transferred to Somerville's A.M.E. church. The early part of the twentieth century in America saw widespread racial prejudice. African Americans who spoke their minds risked being lynched—murdered by a mob—often strung up by a rope thrown over the nearest tree limb or light pole. It happened frequently in the South and the Midwest, and African Americans all across the country realized it could occur wherever they lived, even in a peaceful place like Somerville. Paul and the one other African American in his high school class had to be careful in their conduct. Luckily, Paul had a number of outlets for his youthful energy.

Beginning at the age of fourteen, Paul joined a group of African-American students recruited to work in the resort hotels at Narragansett Pier in Rhode Island. Paul's older brother Ben had worked there for several years, and Paul landed a job as a kitchen helper. His day began at 4:00 A.M. and did not end until dark. While Ben had things comparatively easy as a waiter, Paul scrubbed pots and pans, mopped floors, wiped off tables, hauled supplies, and performed other tiresome or lowly kitchen chores. He spent several summers working in Rhode Island, but only during his first summer did he have to keep pots and pans sparkling in the kitchen.

In high school, Robeson was a member of the debating team and sang with the glee club. He also served as

Paul Robeson, front, played baseball and basketball as a young boy in Westfield, New Jersey, where this photograph of the baseball team was taken.

a study-hall monitor, and he became a dramatic actor whenever it was time to put on a play. He sang in the choir in his father's church, sometimes delivering the Sunday sermon when the Reverend Robeson was ill or out of town. In school, Robeson played the part of Mark Antony in the funeral scene in Shakespeare's *Julius Caesar*. That theatrical event attracted a great deal of attention, in part because the boy playing the murdered Caesar spotted his robe with blobs of ketchup! In his junior year, Paul took the title role in

Shakespeare's tragedy *Othello*. As Othello, Paul proved to be wildly popular with the audience.[5]

Paul was a star on the field, on the stage, and in the classroom. It must have seemed to his high school friends that young Robeson had a corner on talent. His family had always encouraged his singing, and he got lots of practice in his father's church. Once brother Ben and the Reverend Robeson realized how good Paul's voice really was, he became a central figure in the church choir. Besides carrying a tune well, Paul could reach effortlessly for bass notes listeners could almost feel. One day, his stirring voice on such songs as "Ol' Man River" would bring him worldwide renown.

The only African American on the high school football team, Paul initially suffered bruises in practice at the hands of players who wanted the team to remain all white. But the coach realized how good his lone black player was and told the white players that anyone who annoyed Robeson would be off the team. When Somerville played archrival Phillipsburg, Robeson starred in "the greatest game ever played" on Phillipsburg's field, according to the local newspaper.[6] Though Somerville lost that contest, Paul kept his team in the game.

The Reverend Robeson often showed up to watch his son practice or play. He realized that there was a fine line between avoiding confrontation and being an

"Uncle Tom"—that is, yielding to the wishes of whites far beyond what was necessary—and he taught Paul to walk that fine line. Paul was considered intelligent, cooperative, talented, and a good sport. He was called names but hid his anger most of the time. Perhaps because he was an essentially happy and good-natured young man, life was good to him during his high school years. But it was not perfect.

After years of oratory practice in front of his father, Paul entered a statewide speaking contest. The first round took place at his local high school, where he was the best male speaker. White adults judged the contest, and they could scarcely tell one boy from another because all were evenly matched. Then Paul took the stage. Delivering the famed oration of Toussaint L'Ouverture, the black Haitian revolutionary who defeated Napoleon's forces in a rebellion against slavery, Robeson dazzled the crowd. His deep voice boomed out across the auditorium, and he performed without error. Paul said nothing when he was awarded only third place in the contest.

A high school senior in 1915, Paul passed over two potential college choices. Nearby Princeton was an excellent school but was filled with white students from the Deep South and would not admit black students (this policy changed after World War II). The Reverend Robeson wanted Paul to attend his alma mater, Lincoln University in Pennsylvania. But Paul felt that he could compete in a larger, mostly white school. He passed the entrance examination for Rutgers College in New Brunswick, New Jersey. He also took a test that won him a four-year scholarship to Rutgers. Paul felt he had nothing to fear: "I *knew* I was not inferior," he later wrote.[7]

3

COLLEGE AND
MARRIAGE

oday, Rutgers University in New Jersey has thousands of students on large campuses in several cities. But when Paul Robeson entered as a freshman in 1915, it had just one small campus in New Brunswick. The school was all male and had only five hundred students. Robeson was larger than almost anyone else at the school. As one of only two African Americans enrolled, the seventeen-year-old stood out.

Just as in high school, Robeson tried out for the football team. During the first practice, some players piled on the new freshman, breaking his nose, damaging his shoulder, and generally bruising him from

At his first Rutgers College football practice, Robeson was attacked by some of his teammates. Still, it was not long before they learned to respect his outstanding athletic ability.

head to toe. Robeson didn't let on to his teammates how badly he had been hurt after that first practice. But he went back to his room and could scarcely crawl into bed. He did not fully recover for ten days. Nevertheless, he forced himself to continue. He was determined not to take any more abuse. At the next practice, when he was again attacked, Robeson, who usually tried to avoid confrontations, let loose his temper. He picked up the player and held him high overhead, preparing to slam him to the ground.

Luckily for the fellow dangling in midair, the coach stepped in. Coach G. Foster Sanford warned his players that mauling Robeson would not be tolerated and that Paul had made the team. Paul was lucky—the coach had seen him play in high school and was pleased he had decided to attend Rutgers. More important, Coach Sanford was an advocate of racial harmony, a man ahead of his time in the early part of the twentieth century.

After that, Robeson's teammates accepted him. Soon they began to depend on his superior playing to win ball games. Robeson was a wonderful football player on both offense and defense. Despite his ability, however, he was benched for a couple of games because opposing teams refused to compete against an African American. No one knows how many times opponents piled on Robeson just to rough him up. A West Virginia player once threatened to cut out his heart.[1]

Neither threats nor anything else stopped Robeson, who played for four years on the Rutgers football team. Charles Taylor, a sports reporter writing in *The New York Tribune*, covered a game in 1917 between Rutgers and Fordham University. He reported that "Robeson was supposed to play full-back on the defensive, and he did, but never did a full-back range so widely as he. If there was a gap in the line Robeson filled it. If the Rutgers ends were the least bit remiss . . . Robeson was on hand to prevent any

Robeson poses with other star players of the 1918 Rutgers football team.

substantial progress."[2] Writing that same year, another New York reporter called Robeson "the best all-around player on the gridiron this season and the most valuable to the team."[3]

Robeson played four varsity sports—football, baseball, basketball, and track—winning fifteen varsity letters in his years at Rutgers. In the classroom, Robeson, known as "Robey," worked hard. He also tutored other students, competed in debates, and sang in the glee club. He found time to take part-time jobs, including that of a railroad porter in New York City's Grand Central Station. Robeson dated several women. Since there were so few African Americans at Rutgers, many of his friends came from nearby schools such as Teachers Normal School in the larger city of Trenton.

When time permitted, Robeson returned home to visit his father and to sing in the church choir on Sunday mornings. The Reverend Robeson was fascinated by what his son was learning, and he was as keen as ever about encouraging the young man to work even harder. Robeson was an exceptional student, routinely earning 90 percent or higher in his studies, the equivalent of A grades. The Reverend Robeson wondered why the grades weren't 100 percent and was told by his son that no one ever earned a perfect score. "What's one hundred for if nobody ever gets it?" the elder Robeson wanted to know.[4]

Robeson was well known at Rutgers, and not simply

because it was a small school. For two years in a row, sportswriters selected him to the All-America football team. Rutgers professors found it a pleasure to have such a capable student in their classes. In his junior year, Robeson was accepted into Phi Beta Kappa, an exclusive organization for high-achieving college students. This honor was offset by the fact that his beloved father died that year at the age of seventy-three. The elder Robeson had been in ill health for some time, no longer able to deliver his Sunday morning sermons on a regular basis.

Robeson was stunned by his father's death, but he had to go on with his life. He worked in Rhode Island for the summer, he played football in the fall, and he was elected by his classmates to the Cap and Skull senior honor society. Cap and Skull recognized the four students who best represented the ideals of Rutgers. Robeson was also named the valedictorian— the student with the highest grades—of his graduating class. Asked to speak at his graduation in 1919, Robeson received a standing ovation from teachers and students as he walked down the aisle. After all, he had focused nationwide attention on Rutgers with his ability on the playing field.

Robeson's graduation speech mixed patriotic, racial, and religious themes. He praised the United States for being the cradle of liberty, noting that the nation was an ideal place for the "less favored race" to

Each year, four Rutgers seniors were elected by their classmates to the Cap and Skull honor society. Paul Robeson was very proud to be chosen.

grow and prosper.[5] He reminded the white majority to show compassion as African Americans worked their way up the ladder. He ended with a call for a day when "black and white shall clasp friendly hands" under God.[6] Applause for Robeson's dramatic delivery was long and loud. Robeson's words showed how he felt and, sadly, that many black people at the time had been convinced by white people that they were inferior.

After graduating from Rutgers, Robeson was accepted into law school at New York University in New York City. He moved to Harlem, a section of the city, and found a job to earn money for law school in the fall. He could hardly have picked a better place to be at the time: Harlem was about to enjoy an incredible burst of artistic creativity. Originally a wealthy area of white merchants, Harlem in 1919 was growing increasingly black. Many of the African Americans who migrated there were musicians, actors, writers, or artists. They were joined by a small but noticeable group of blacks from the Caribbean and from Africa.

The recent Rutgers graduate fit right in. Robeson was ambitious and well known, ready for law school but also prepared for any other opportunity that came his way. He was handsome and carried himself well. When he walked down the street, people noticed. Because of his athletic accomplishments, he was widely known; he was "one of the boys," an elite group of promising young men.[7] Robeson moved in with a couple of young musician friends and earned extra money singing at parties and other social affairs of wealthy white people. A resident or frequent visitor to Harlem for most of his life, Robeson was instantly recognizable by sight or even by voice.

The average Harlem resident was extremely aware of race and the subtle ways in which the majority looked down on black citizens. For example, Robeson was urged by some black activists not to sing traditional Negro spirituals. Despite their popularity, the songs reminded black and white listeners alike of the slavery, poverty, and humiliation that were aspects of African-American history. As good-natured as his voice was deep, Robeson usually sang whatever was requested and knew a large number of spirituals and other tunes by heart. Through it all, his voice emerged triumphant, bigger than Robeson himself. Over the years, many who heard Robeson's voice for the first time, live or recorded, could later remember not only the song but the time and the place.

Robeson began law school at New York University but soon decided to transfer to Columbia University for his second semester.[8] Robeson earned some of his tuition money tutoring Coach Sanford's son in Latin. He also continued to be an exceptional athlete and in the fall of 1919 spent several weekends playing professional football. Robeson played for the Akron Pros and then the Milwaukee Badgers, riding long hours on the train to reach his Midwest games. Though he was sometimes turned away when teammates entered a restaurant or stayed in a hotel that would not admit African Americans, Robeson earned as much as $1,000 per game—a huge amount of money at the time.

Robeson also helped the football coaches at Rutgers and at Lincoln University in Philadelphia, where his father had gone to college. Paid very little, Robeson accepted the Lincoln position because he enjoyed the people at the school. Lincoln students were aware that Robeson was a former All-American football star, and they quickly inducted him into a social fraternity. Parties often followed football practice, and Robeson had fond memories of the time spent with his friends from Lincoln.

Robeson suffered an injury that could have cost him his life during one of the brutal professional games that were played at that time in flimsy helmets and uniforms with almost no padding. He hobbled off the train when he returned to New York City and made his way to Presbyterian Hospital, nursing a leg injury. Doctors examined the athlete and were stunned to find a gouge in Robeson's thigh muscle. What had begun as a routine hospital visit turned into major surgery. The football player was confined to bed for several weeks. Always popular, he had numerous visitors during his recovery. Among them was a young hospital employee named Eslanda Cardozo Goode.

Robeson injured his leg playing in a professional football game. At that time, football players wore flimsy helmets and uniforms with little padding.

"Essie," like Robeson's mother, was descended from people considered higher class. She could trace her family tree back to a Spanish-Jewish man who secretly married a slave in Charleston, South Carolina, about the time of the Revolutionary War. The couple's descendants were well educated.

Essie's father had died when she was very young. Her mother studied medicine and chemistry, creating a successful line of beauty and skin-care products. The family settled in Chicago, where Essie graduated from high school at the age of sixteen and won a four-year scholarship to the University of Illinois. She was bright and popular in college, majoring in chemistry. She was chosen for membership in a sorority of elite young black women. Following graduation in 1917, she took a job as a chemist at Presbyterian Hospital.

Robeson, lying in pain in his hospital bed, was far less nervous than Essie Goode when the two were introduced by a physician. Their personalities seemed almost exact opposites. The patient was thoughtful, happy, and relaxed. The woman who stood at the end of his bed was high-strung, almost crackling with nervous energy. She wanted to please Robeson, but he merely wanted to be himself.[9]

The lanky football player regained his strength and checked out of the hospital. Essie Goode learned that Robeson was in love with someone else. But the other woman, Gerry Neale, told Robeson that she was more interested in a career than in marriage. Robeson heard that Essie had been seen around town with a handsome young man named Grant Lucas. Realizing he did not want to lose her, Robeson had a change of heart. He visited Essie and asked her to marry him.

Robeson and his betrothed hopped on a train and headed for Connecticut, where they believed they could be married very quickly. They found instead that they would have to wait five days for a license because they were out-of-state residents. So they took the train back to New York State. When the locomotive stopped in the small town of Port Chester, New York, Robeson noticed the town clerk's office nearby. The two young people were married by the local public official in a few minutes and caught a later train into New York City.

The Robesons did not immediately tell anyone about their marriage or live together. Both had roommates, and neither one could afford to make new living arrangements. Paul in particular was scraping for money. Essie had a bit more and began to look for items for their first home. They soon moved into the top floor of a house with furniture purchased on the installment plan, which meant that they could pay just a small amount each month. Robeson quickly learned that marriage would be very different from bachelor life.

Mrs. Robeson didn't care for the casual way her husband dressed. She threw out some of his things, bought a few others, and was quick to tell Paul when he looked good—and when he did not. She was an early riser; he scheduled afternoon classes so that he could sleep late. Such behavior drove her crazy. She rolled him out of bed every day at 7:00 A.M. He waited until she went to work, then returned to bed until noon. Robeson needed sleep because he was a full-time student and part-time athlete, plus he performed late-night singing engagements whenever he could.

During his second year of law school, Robeson accepted his first professional stage part. The play was *Taboo*, and Paul would play a wandering minstrel. He was not sure about acting in the play, but Essie was insistent.[10] She felt that her handsome husband might have a career in show business rather than in law, and she was always looking for opportunities. The play was a musical melodrama, set in Louisiana before the Civil War. The New York critics enjoyed Robeson and his hypnotic voice, but they hated the play.

Taboo closed just as Robeson's second year of law school ended, and he found himself without much to do. Another show was looking for a singer with a bass voice, and Robeson joined the cast of a much better musical, *Shuffle Along*. After just a few shows, the author of *Taboo* offered Robeson the chance to perform his *Taboo* role in England. Encouraged by his wife, the young vocalist joined the entire cast of *Taboo*, now renamed *Voodoo*, in sailing across the Atlantic Ocean in 1922.

While in law school at Columbia University in New York City, Robeson secretly married Eslanda Goode. She encouraged him to accept his first professional stage part.

Essie became desperately ill right after Robeson departed. A physician examined her and said that she needed surgery related to an earlier appendectomy. Despite her pain, she wrote Robeson a number of letters and gave them to a friend. The friend mailed one letter each day, making it appear that all was well. Robeson wrote back faithfully every day.

Being apart was not easy for either of them. The musical opened in Blackpool, England, and was no more well received there than it had been in New York. Robeson was initially enthusiastic, then concerned. He considered staying in England and studying for a year at Oxford. He devoted a letter to that question, asking Essie her opinion. Happily, after the cool reception in Blackpool, *Voodoo* was greeted more warmly in Glasgow, Scotland. Robeson's mood improved.

That changed with the receipt of a letter from his wife. After being in the hospital for a month, she had begun to wonder if she would ever recover. She now told Robeson the truth, admitting that her previous chatty letters had been written before her hospital stay. The entertainer read his wife's news with great concern and sailed home as soon as he could.[11] Two weeks after their emotional bedside reunion, Essie was able to return to her husband in their apartment.

By his final year of law school, Robeson realized that he did not care all that much about being an attorney.[12] His grades were not high—they were just good enough to graduate, in part because he was also busy working and performing whenever he could. Equally important, a brief experience working in a major New York law firm revealed a depressing truth: White people did not want a black lawyer handling their affairs. Even more demeaning, a white secretary refused to work for him simply because he was black.

Years later, Robeson remembered this period in his life quite fondly:

> At this time I was an aspiring lawyer, believing that to succeed would help raise my people, the Black people of the world. Theater and concerts were furthest from my mind; this [trip to England] was just a lark. Instead of waiting on tables in hotels to earn money, I was being paid twenty pounds or so a week for expenses to walk on stage, say a few lines, sing a song or two. Just too good for words.[13]

All the while, the former football player was making theatrical contacts. In the fall of 1923, he learned that one of America's great playwrights, Eugene O'Neill, had written a new play with believable black characters. *All God's Chillun Got Wings* was to be presented in New York City by a group called the Provincetown Players, and Robeson auditioned for it. He read the lines and won a part, impressing fellow cast members. From that moment on, Robeson would never again enter a classroom as a student or enter an office as a practicing attorney. He was in show business.

4

SHOW BUSINESS

T he year 1924 was an extraordinarily busy one for Paul Robeson. A recording company wanted him to sing for its label. A Chicago theatrical company tried to lure him away from the Provincetown Players. A famous artist wanted to make a sculpture of him. Perhaps most impressive, the tall, handsome singer was cast in an all-black movie, *Body and Soul*, and the producers promised him additional money if the film did well. Robeson never bothered to take the bar examination, which would have allowed him to practice law in the state of New York.

Shortly before rehearsals began for *All God's Chillun*

Robeson found himself in demand as a singer and actor.

Got Wings, Robeson played the part of a sinful black preacher in a revival of *Roseanne*. The only remarkable aspect of this performance was that before Robeson, only white men whose faces were covered with black makeup had played this part. Just as women were portrayed by men in Shakespeare's time, in the 1920s minorities rarely performed in the theater, even to play ethnic characters. Robeson helped change all that.

Roseanne had an all-black cast. The play was critically acclaimed, and while the crowds were enthusiastic, they were small. Several reviewers noted Robeson's talent and said they could not wait to see him in *Chillun*. Some said he would make a good lead in O'Neill's *The Emperor Jones*, which he soon proved true. Meanwhile, reaction was mounting in the New York newspapers to the fact that *Chillun* would star a black man and a white woman.

The scene that stirred emotions involved Robeson's hand being kissed by the white actress playing opposite him. Playwright O'Neill and several others defended the script, claiming that people had judged the play without reading it. That wasn't true—those who objected said they had read the play and disliked the story. O'Neill did not want to risk calling major newspapers prejudiced, since he and the Provincetown Players depended on favorable reviews from newspaper critics. Reviews of *Chillun*, performed in New York City as originally written, were indeed positive.

The 1920s was a wonderful period for the arts. Commercial radio broadcasting began in 1920, bringing entertainment into homes wherever there was electricity to power a large clunky receiver. The first movie with sound was made in 1923, and the following year George Gershwin wrote *Rhapsody in Blue*, a hypnotic mix of jazz and classical music. Al Jolson appeared in *The Jazz Singer*, a popular movie in 1927, and the musical *Show Boat* opened later that same year in New York City.

Meanwhile, in Greenwich Village in New York City, the arts were livelier than ever. Theater, music, dance, and writing were treated to an African-American spin that was original, sometimes breathtakingly brilliant. Not everything being done was flamboyant. In fact, Robeson took advantage of a friend's subtle talent to become more widely known than he could have dreamed.

That friend was Laurence Brown, a skilled African-American pianist the Robesons first met during the production of *Voodoo* in England. Brown and Robeson began to practice Negro spirituals, the religious songs of slaves. These historic songs, such as "Swing Low, Sweet Chariot," were arranged by Brown in a unique way. Robeson's bass-baritone voice made them memorable. Brown "guided me to the beauty of our own folk music," Robeson would later recall.[1]

Robeson and Brown had become acquainted by

chance in England. The pianist impressed Robeson with his good manners and the fact that he was intelligent and widely read. More important, the singer was convinced by Brown that Negro spirituals were a great form of expression.[2]

Brown and Robeson tried the songs on friends and found them visibly moved. Audiences grew bigger and demanded more spirituals, despite the fact that many African Americans wanted only to forget the slavery and oppression from which the songs came. Robeson sang sixteen songs one evening in a Greenwich Village theater and ended up doing sixteen more songs for encores. People continued to stomp, clap, and cheer for several minutes after the performance finally ended.

Demands for the songs, the voice, and the man poured in from across the United States. The Victor Talking Machine Company (later named RCA) signed Robeson to an exclusive one-year recording contract that guaranteed him four records. The singer posed for pictures that ran in *Vanity Fair*, a fashionable magazine. Mr. and Mrs. Robeson rubbed elbows with celebrities, almost all of whom were white and most of whom were cordial. Robeson became the first concert singer to present programs in which all songs were written by African Americans—and blacks and whites liked what they heard.

No matter how famous or talented Robeson

When Paul Robeson sang, people listened, for the sound of his deep voice was magic. Over the years he toured many times with his accompanist Lawrence Brown.

became, however, there were slights. For instance, he and Larry Brown were invited to sing at an artists' and writers' club, where an appearance made guests automatic honorary members. A British explorer was inducted into the club that same day, but Robeson and Brown were not. Both said they were treated well, but they had, nevertheless, been snubbed.

About the same time, *The Emperor Jones* was to be performed in London. Robeson successfully auditioned for the show. It may have been with relief that he and Essie sailed for England in August 1925. Despite Robeson's string of critical successes, the couple had to borrow several thousand dollars from a white patron of the arts in order to pay bills and have money to live before the play began. Robeson gave several financially successful concerts just before departing.

Essie was convinced that England was less prejudiced than the United States. The truth was, England had very few persons of African descent, so racial matters were not much of an issue. The Robesons were a novelty and could walk or ride anywhere, eating and shopping where they chose. The entertainer would later recall, "I was treated as a gentleman and a scholar."[3] Such treatment made Robeson believe he could, with his music, reach his goals of personal satisfaction and service to his people.[4]

Robeson wowed audiences and critics in *The*

Emperor Jones. The day after his first performance, he gave six interviews by midafternoon. London was a city with many large-circulation newspapers, and they uniformly praised not only Robeson's voice but also his acting ability and his mere presence on the stage. In the very center of London, his name was etched in lights at a major intersection.

The Robesons returned in 1926 to the United States, and Paul Robeson and Larry Brown were booked for their first United States concert tour. Meanwhile, the Robesons were not getting along as well as they once had. Besides being his wife, Essie had become the manager of Robeson's career. So when Robeson lent someone money or failed to show up somewhere promptly or stayed out late with friends, she confronted him. Mrs. Robeson had her husband's best interests in mind. On the other hand, her protective attitude toward her "star" often created problems between the two of them. At one point, the singer left home and did not return for two weeks.

Yet the Robesons always seemed to hit it off when a promising part came along, and one came along later that year. Robeson won the lead role in *Black Boy*, a play based on the rise and fall of the famed African-American heavyweight boxer Jack Johnson. Once again, reviews of the play were mixed, while the reviews of Robeson's performance were very positive. Robeson and Essie wondered when, and if, the next

In the 1920s and 1930s, Robeson frequently starred in *The Emperor Jones,* by playwright Eugene O'Neill.

good part in a good play would come along. Or was it impossible for a play featuring a black character to be well received in the United States in the 1920s?

Robeson put such thoughts aside for several reasons. After years of hoping, Essie was excited to learn that she was pregnant. Robeson, however, soon announced that he was going on a concert tour of Europe. The tour would have him out of the country when the baby was due. Essie encouraged her husband to make the tour for the sake of the money and the prestige. Once again she bade the entertainer adieu from the dock of a steamship company.

A healthy son, Paul Robeson, Jr., was born November 2, 1927. Unfortunately, Essie experienced several complications from childbirth. She spent another long period in the hospital, again minimizing her problems in letters to her husband. It was not until Essie's mother wrote to Robeson that he found out the seriousness of his wife's condition. He sailed home to be with her. Several weeks later, she was well enough to resume managing his career.

The Robesons began to worry that Paul's career was in trouble. For example, Robeson turned down a part in a play that went on to win a Pulitzer Prize. He became convinced that he could improve his situation by broadening his appeal. One way to do this might be to audition for opera, which had not interested him at all in the past. However, there were few parts for a black man and the demands of opera would have strained his deep but fragile voice. Robeson's career did not move in that direction.

Other disappointments followed, among them a movie deal that never happened and offers for singing parts that Robeson either disliked or that did not suit his voice and style. Luckily, the entertainer was offered a part in the London production of *Show Boat*. (Paul Jr. at first stayed behind with Essie's mother.) Larry Brown came to London, and the vocalist and pianist gave concerts of spirituals on Sundays, Robeson's day off. Paul and Essie Robeson would consider London their home for the next twelve years.

Show Boat made Robeson famous for his rendition of "Ol' Man River." The song became his virtual trademark—no one before or after was able to sing it so richly. Equally important, *Show Boat* was wildly popular with audiences, in part because it had dozens of actors and actresses, eighteen scenes, and highly romantic music. Except for a few African-American critics who said the musical stereotyped blacks, the favorable reception was widespread. In fact, the show created great demand for Robeson-and-Brown concerts.

One problem loomed on the horizon for Robeson. Back in January 1928, he had accepted some money after signing an agreement to appear in a musical review in the United States. Before the review began rehearsals, the singer had sailed to England to be in

Show Boat. Now the people behind the musical review wanted to punish Robeson for failing to honor his contract. The Robesons were living well in London, and they had sent for her mother and Paul Jr. They were spending English pounds as fast as they earned them. At the same time, the arts patron who had lent them $5,000 several years earlier wanted his loan repaid.

Essie tried to deal with the contract matter in a series of letters. Eventually, the matter with the musical review people was settled out of court. Robeson had to appease them because he was threatened with suspension from Actors' Equity, the union that usually made sure actors were paid but also made them honor their agreements.

During his spare time, Robeson found that he had a natural gift for learning foreign languages and began to study French and German. He took singing lessons, feeling that this was one way to maintain the quality of his voice. And he became fascinated with the folk music of Russia, seeing in it sentiments similar to those found in the songs of his African heritage.

Essie busied herself with writing. A major New York publisher wanted a biography of her husband. After her first draft was complete, she showed it to an American friend. He advised removing herself from the work so that it would read more like a standard biography. She made some revisions and sent the book

Paul Robeson

The musical *Show Boat* was wildly successful, and Robeson became famous for his rich rendition of the song "Ol' Man River."

to America, where it would be published in 1930 as *Paul Robeson, Negro*. Sales were mediocre.

About the same time, Robeson experienced a form of discrimination that he had experienced in the United States but not in England. He was supposed to meet a friend for a late-evening drink in the snazzy Savoy Hotel restaurant. When he arrived, he was told by a waiter that blacks were no longer permitted there. Robeson called the manager, who confirmed that blacks had indeed recently been banished. The irony was that the Robesons had dined in the restaurant many times.

Returning to the United States, the singer blamed the Savoy incident on the influence of American racial ideas. Simultaneously, he began his most ambitious singing tour of his native land. Despite visiting many areas with negative attitudes toward blacks, Robeson found that critics and audiences were solidly behind him. At one stop, Carnegie Hall in New York City, the big-city critics were hard on him. But the audience was extremely responsive, and he was able to fill the hall for two concerts within five days.

All the while, Robeson studied *Othello*, the classic Shakespeare play. The hero, for whom the play is named, is an African general who marries a beautiful Italian woman named Desdemona. Othello grows incredibly jealous of his wife because he believes she is seeing other men. The fires of jealousy are fueled by the evil Iago, who spreads rumors to the warrior. Othello eventually kills his wife, despite her complete innocence. Paul Robeson starred as Othello in London in 1930, but the show had only a brief run. A little more than a decade later, in 1943, Robeson would play this role on Broadway to great acclaim.

5

AFRICA AND THE SOVIET UNION

aul and Essie Robeson were not typical Americans—or typical African Americans, for that matter. While many Americans lost their jobs and suffered during the Great Depression, the Robesons sailed back and forth in luxury between the United States and Europe. Paul continued his busy acting and concert career, and Essie continued as his manager. It was a mark of Robeson's talent that the two could prosper as roving entertainer and manager.

Not that the two were always happy. Robeson stayed out late or stayed away when he felt like it, and Essie felt that he had no fatherly feeling toward little Paul.[1] The child lived for several years in Switzerland or in New York City with Essie's mother, because of his parents' hectic schedule. Paul Jr. saw his parents only occasionally as they traveled back and forth for singing engagements.

Robeson returned to America in 1932 for a magnificent New York production of *Show Boat*. Critics gushed over the large, star-studded cast, and they were even more taken with Robeson, who played the part of Joe. His voice, his stage presence, his dramatic ability—there was something about the man that riveted the eyes of the audience whenever he came on stage. Essie did not see or hear the praise firsthand because she stayed behind in London.

The good fortune continued a few months later when he was awarded an honorary master of arts degree by Rutgers University. Robeson attracted crowds whenever he went to Harlem to visit old friends. It is hardly an exaggeration to state that he was, until Joe Louis became the heavyweight boxing champion in 1937, the best-known black man in America. He returned to London in January 1933 for another production of *All God's Chillun*.

Robeson met a number of educated, politically active Africans in London who impressed him. They were fighting colonialism—the rule of one country by another—and he became sympathetic to their cause. Africa at the time was run by several colonial powers: Belgium, England, France, Italy, Portugal, and Spain. Africans were not allowed a say in their form of government. They were kept poor and ill-educated and were mistreated. The Soviet Union spoke out against colonialism, and Robeson was drawn to the Soviet form of government, which was communism. Communists believe, among other things, that all property should be shared.

Along with his increased knowledge of Africa came criticism of American life. Robeson believed that what made American culture different from European culture was the African-American thread that ran through it. He felt a duty to produce plays and movies that connected African history with the world's great civilizations, from the Chinese to the Jews.[2] He became a student once again, this time at London University. He studied the various languages of the West African coast, speaking several with fluency in only a matter of weeks.

Besides improving his delivery of African folk songs, the languages strengthened Robeson's beliefs. He began to see African songs and history as a means of uplifting American blacks. Robeson realized that both Africans and American blacks had been convinced of their inferiority by white people. Black people were different, not inferior. He worried that Africans would throw away their heritage in their efforts to modernize. He wanted to preserve that heritage.[3]

Robeson learned to speak several African languages. He saw African folk songs and history as a means of uplifting American blacks.

The former college football star ran the risk of being misinterpreted. American newspaper reporters seemed especially eager to take what Robeson said and bend it in such a way that it would anger white readers. He grew tired of this, longing at various times to settle down somewhere in Africa where there would be no "burden of my race."[4] But Robeson loved the stage, and there was never any danger of his premature retirement.

Sometimes, Robeson made up his mind a little too quickly. Like many residents of Harlem at the time, he did not care for jazz. Shrugging off its originality, he said it was less pure than African music and that it had been influenced as much by Broadway as by the experience of American blacks. Like many black intellectuals, Robeson later came to realize that Count Basie, Ella Fitzgerald, Dizzy Gillespie, Thelonious Monk, Charlie Parker, and others were creating their own form of genius. He came to see Negro folk music as having an "immense influence" on jazz.[5]

Meanwhile, the entertainer was admired worldwide. One distant admirer was the critically acclaimed Soviet filmmaker Sergei Eisenstein. In 1934, Eisenstein wanted to make a movie about nineteenth-century Haitian blacks and their successful efforts against the French to overthrow colonialism. Eisenstein wanted Robeson to be his star.

The Robesons were invited to the Soviet Union and

jumped at the chance. They crossed the English Channel and boarded a train for the long ride eastward, through Europe to Moscow. The couple spent a night in Berlin, where they met a Jewish friend who warned that the Nazis were turning Germany into a horrible place. Seeing the threatening German military presence helped strengthen Robeson's preference for the Soviet Union. Viewing the Nazis, Robeson noted, "was like seeing the Ku Klux Klan in power."[6]

Robeson dazzled the Soviets with his ability to speak Russian. Likewise, his concerts were extremely well received. He was introduced to all the important people, including the dictator Joseph Stalin. Robeson was quizzed by Americans who had moved to Moscow and by Soviet citizens concerning the arts and current events in the United States.

One popular topic in the Soviet Union was the plight of the "Scottsboro Boys." Nine young African Americans, ranging in age from thirteen to twenty-one, were accused in 1931 of raping two white women on a train outside Paint Rock, Alabama. The "Scottsboro Nine" were tried and convicted, despite the fact that none of them had adequate legal counsel. An all-white jury sentenced all but one of them to death.

The case was taken up by black organizations such as the National Association for the Advancement of Colored People (NAACP). It also became the focus of a number of national and international organizations, including the Communist Party of the United States. NAACP leaders were skeptical of the motives of the Communists, believing the accused young men were being used for propaganda purposes. On the other hand, many blacks became more sympathetic to radical political movements. African Americans saw the importance of politics and protest in the struggle for social change.

The case of the Scottsboro Boys had a strong impact on Paul Robeson for other reasons as well. It showed that Communists were eager to recruit American blacks. And it was one more indication that an African American did not stand much of a chance for equal treatment in the United States. The world appeared to be choosing up sides in the 1930s, and Robeson grew more and more likely to take the Communist view.[7]

Robeson stayed busy professionally. In quick succession he took the lead role of the Haitian hero in *Toussaint L'Ouverture* in a London stage play and the part of Joe in the Hollywood film version of *Show Boat*. All the while, he weighed two issues that were important to him: politics and race. Politics was important because it could be used to free oppressed black people. Race was crucial because African Americans played down their link with Africa, making anything African seem automatically inferior.

The chance to play an African as he should be played came to Robeson in very few movies. One was *Song of Freedom*. Unlike other films, in which Paul played primitive, scheming, or shuffling blacks, this film showed him as an intelligent man. The story is about a black dockworker in London who discovers through his singing career that he is an African king. Robeson referred to *Song of Freedom* in later years as one of his favorite films.[8]

Robeson returned to the Soviet Union briefly, this time with Essie's mother and his son. The entertainer enrolled Paul Jr. in school in Moscow, believing that there he would be free of racial prejudice. About the same time, Essie made a grand tour of Africa, perhaps to heighten her interest in something to which her husband was devoted. Robeson went to Hollywood for more moviemaking, including such popular films as *King Solomon's Mines*.

By the late 1930s, Robeson had soured on motion pictures. "They [the industry] will never let me play a part in a film in which a Negro is on top," he told a London interviewer. A year earlier, in 1937, he lamented, "One man can't face the film companies. . . . So no more films for me."[9]

Having covered a good part of the earth traveling from one performance to the next, Robeson found his political views taking shape. By the fall of 1937, with civil wars under way in China and Spain, Robeson

Robeson takes a break to study the musical score on the set of *Song of Freedom,* one of his favorite films.

emerged as a political spokesperson. He used his songs in London during a rally to win over his audience. With his wonderful voice, he was a beacon of talent among Socialists and Communists.

Fearing the growing power of Germany under the dictator Adolf Hitler, Robeson told a London radio audience, "Every artist, every scientist, must decide now where he stands. . . . The battlefront is everywhere."[10] He saw any willingness to appease Hitler as only enabling more of Europe to come under the dictator's rule. Robeson returned to the United States in 1939 primarily, he said, "to be among the Negro people during the great world crisis that was looming."[11]

6

ACTIVISM

The warning came from an English business associate of Paul Robeson's, and it was not subtle: If the entertainer did not keep his political thoughts to himself, he would endanger his career. Happily, for his numerous supporters, Robeson did not listen to the advice. In fact, he became more of an activist with each passing year in the late 1930s.

A "major turning point" for Robeson came in December 1937 when he decided to go to Spain.[1] There, army officers under Generalissimo Francisco Franco had revolted against the Republican government. In a civil war that would last three years and claim one million lives, Franco was supported by Nazi

Germany and fascist Italy. Opposing the military was a loose confederation of Loyalists (backers of the government): Socialists, Communists, Democrats, and Republicans. From the start, the Loyalist side was greatly outgunned.

Many people with strong convictions from Europe and North America went to Spain to fight for the Loyalist side. Included were a number of African Americans who were willing to put their lives on the line to battle fascism (dictatorship government). On their 1938 visit, the Robesons met several such men and were impressed with their courage. Dodging bombs and artillery, the Robesons took a whirlwind tour of Spain. They traveled in a large car and stayed in old and luxurious hotels in bomb-ravaged cities.

It must have been a strange sight for Loyalist soldiers. They turned away from the front lines to see an African American step out of a shiny sedan and break into song. If they did not recognize the man, they recognized his tunes, for Paul Robeson was known all over Europe. In turn, Robeson was in awe of people like Oliver Law, a young African American from Chicago whose skill in battle elevated him to the rank of commandant just before he was killed.

Robeson noted that the quick tour of Spain made "a great impression."[2] He had never met so many people risking death to fight against overwhelming odds for a just cause. Nor had he ever met so many tough, well-armed people who loved his music. Among them were several young African Americans, not all of whom would survive the conflict. Remarkably, soldiers on both sides in a battle once stopped fighting for an hour-long truce just so everyone could gather to hear Robeson sing! His voice carried among the bomb-scarred and bullet-riddled buildings.

Though never officially a Communist himself, Robeson met Earl Browder, head of the American Communist Party, while in Spain. Communists world-wide feared a fascist takeover wherever it might occur. Robeson increasingly began to see the coming conflict as one in which fascist Germany would be on one side and the Communist Soviet Union would be on the other. Which side would the United States choose?

Like a number of Americans, Robeson sometimes turned a blind eye to the evils of international communism. He did have strong feelings about the trials that were going on in the Soviet Union at the time. Soviet dictator Joseph Stalin was getting rid of any citizens he considered a threat. Consequently, all sorts of people, from veteran army generals to young artists, were being shot by firing squads or sent into lifelong slave labor. Asked by the press about such activity, Robeson said little about these purges.[3] On the other hand, he quietly pulled his son and Essie's mother out of Moscow.

Robeson was not so quiet about the roles he had

Paul Robeson

As he traveled all over the world to perform, Robeson found his political views taking shape. He was never afraid to express his opinions, even when they got him into trouble.

played in past films. Returning to London, Robeson complained that the parts had all been demeaning. It is true that many of the roles showed black people as shiftless or lazy or mindlessly good-natured. One play in which Robeson found meaning was *Plant in the Sun*, written by a young American, Ben Bengal, which was about to be staged in 1938 in London. The story told of black and white workers joining forces to stage a strike. Their work stoppage helped them obtain justice from the uncaring owner of a factory. Robeson accepted a role and found that many of the minor parts were filled with real laborers.

Robeson threw himself into rehearsals with enthusiasm. He continued to appear without charge for a number of causes. Besides crusading for a free Spain, Robeson spoke on behalf of colonial people in Jamaica and in India. Both were ruled by the British, and the African-American actor believed the color of his skin gave him a special sensitivity. He was warmly received wherever he showed up, and famous Indians, such as independence advocate Jawaharlal Nehru, became his friends.

Plant in the Sun closed in the fall of 1938, and Robeson and Larry Brown took off on another very successful concert tour of Great Britain. Rural English audiences enjoyed both Robeson's voice and his activism. They were aware that he felt a special sympathy for out-of-work Welsh miners and others who had struggled in poverty through the decade. Crowds in Glasgow, Scotland, and southward were turned away at the box office, where Sold Out signs went up early and often. Robeson was seen as a famous recording artist and a great film star.

Based in part on his overwhelming popularity among English listeners and viewers, Robeson planned a tour of Australia. His trip was canceled because the world appeared to be headed for war. Arriving back in the United States, Robeson observed several changes. A national minimum wage had been enacted, the armed forces were being built up, and almost every home had a large Emerson, General Electric, or RCA Victor radio. Cars were equipped with radios, too, mostly Motorolas. Like residents of Great Britain, Americans turned to the radio each evening for news and entertainment.

By his fortieth birthday, in 1938, Robeson had reached the point where he did not have to take a job simply because it paid well. He wanted to choose only the singing obligations or the stage or movie roles he liked, often for political reasons.[4] He appeared in a successful, weeklong revival of *The Emperor Jones* and he met with musical genius Oscar Hammerstein II to discuss the possibility of doing a musical about John Henry, the legendary black man who outworked a machine and died for his efforts.

Far from having been forgotten while in Europe and

At the peak of his career, adoring fans all around the world clamored for Robeson's autograph.

in Great Britain, Robeson was in huge demand in the United States. He sometimes hid from prying reporters, a practice that managed to insult close friends who also could not locate him. It's hardly an exaggeration to state that every time he opened the door, a new offer presented itself. One person wanted him to star in a blues opera, another sought him out for a play about Africa, and another wanted a commitment from the singer for a long-term recording contract.

Robeson was persuaded to return to making movies by the script for *The Proud Valley*. This tale told of an unemployed black man who is hired to work in a Welsh mine. He shares what he has with fellow miners and their down-and-out families. Robeson prepared for the role by losing weight at a health spa. Shortly after shooting began in London, events in Europe distracted Robeson and most other Americans.

England hastily prepared for war. Essie's mother returned to the United States while Essie and Paul Jr. waited impatiently in England for Robeson to finish *The Proud Valley*. Once it was complete, they packed a decade's worth of clothing, furniture, and memories and returned to the United States. Robeson was met by several reporters, who inquired about his feelings concerning world events. Never without an opinion, the singer-actor said the war was not about democracy but was instead about trying to save the German people from their terrible leadership.[5]

Robeson's views were interpreted as isolationist, as discouraging blacks or the United States from taking sides in a war that pitted fascism against communism. The entertainer caused a real stir in England, where arrangements were already under way for the United States to provide supplies, should the Germans attack. There were many Americans who considered themselves isolationists—believing that the United States had no business in the war on either side. In fact, until the United States entered the war, isolationism was a fairly popular stance.

Robeson had plenty of work. He participated in a radio show in November 1939, receiving rave reviews for his rendition of patriotic songs. Once again he opened in a Broadway show, *John Henry*, that got bad reviews but displayed his remarkable talents to good advantage. He also received an honorary degree from Hamilton College in Upstate New York for his contributions to civilization.

Equally important for Robeson, *The Proud Valley* was released in 1940. The film was greeted with lukewarm reviews. Some black activists believed the picture was a step backward because Robeson's character was a marginal one. Through it all, Robeson was applauded for his performance. The film proved, among other things, that the entertainer did not have to sing to be well received.

While Robeson was busy performing, Essie purchased a luxury estate in rural Connecticut in 1941. It had a dozen rooms, a swimming pool, and servants' quarters. The home was lavish, but it hardly met Robeson's needs. His work was centered in New York, so he found an apartment in Greenwich Village that he shared with a sculptor.

Robeson kept a constant eye on current events, despite his hectic show-business schedule. The United States had sentenced Earl Browder, head of the American Communist Party, to prison. Browder was convicted of violating passport rules, but Robeson and others felt he was being silenced for the strong positions he and his party took about war in Europe. The singer attended a "Free Earl Browder" rally in Madison Square Garden, where he called the American Communist leader "the vanguard of the cohorts against fascism."[6]

Americans of all political persuasions were shocked when, on June 22, 1941, Germany invaded the Soviet Union. Opinion in the United States swung strongly against Germany. Paul Robeson's views became more mainstream, as he and the average citizen pulled for Soviet soldiers to somehow stop the crushing Nazi war machine. The entertainer spoke movingly on behalf of the Soviets, asking the administration of President

Franklin D. Roosevelt to provide massive aid. He was joined in the effort by many celebrities while conservative Americans remained silent.

Many people in the powerful white establishment resented show-business activists like Robeson, but none was stronger than J. Edgar Hoover, director of the Federal Bureau of Investigation. Prior to World War II, Hoover had become well known for his crusade against organized crime. As the United States edged toward involvement in the Second World War, Hoover and his FBI agents turned their attention to global politics, with an emphasis on rooting out subversives in America. The director did not like what Paul Robeson was saying and decided to do something about it.

7

UNDER SCRUTINY

he United States entered World War II on December 8, 1941, the day after Japanese planes attacked the United States naval base at Pearl Harbor in the Hawaiian Islands. Most Americans had been less concerned with Japan and Asia than with Germany and Europe. The Soviet Union would begin to push the German Army back toward Berlin late in 1942.

While the United States and the Soviet Union were now on the same side in the war, many Americans distrusted the Communist nation. Among the most suspicious was FBI director J. Edgar Hoover. He did not care for Americans who said positive things about the Soviets. Hoover decided that Paul Robeson must be a member of the Communist Party. Robeson neither admitted nor denied party membership. For years Hoover had the entertainer and his acquaintances followed and spied upon, in public and in private.

The agents' work was cut out for them. Robeson never did become a member of the Communist Party, though he had visited and praised the Soviet Union before the start of World War II. The whole situation today seems laughable: As Robeson participated in public, patriotic rallies that included Americans of all political persuasions, FBI agents wrote down every word he spoke or sang.

Agents also planted electronic listening devices, or "bugs," in apartments and hotel rooms wherever Robeson visited or was staying. Despite the lack of solid evidence, the FBI file on the singer-actor grew thicker and thicker. Hoover saw Robeson as dangerous, deciding to lock him up if martial law ever were declared in the country.[1] Ironically, Robeson's patriotic activities allowed him to get to know Franklin D. Roosevelt's wife, Eleanor, and several of the president's closest friends and advisors. They might have been shocked by anyone who would label the entertainer a Communist.

Robeson and the few Communists active in the United States split on at least one crucial point. The Communists often told black people not to participate in the war, that they were being used by the capitalist system. In contrast, Robeson urged his fellow African Americans to do everything they could to win the war. He did so because he realized that a victory for fascism would mean the kind of treatment of blacks that Jews and others were facing in concentration camps.

As it turned out, America greatly needed the help of its African-American citizens during the war. In Detroit, for example, where the war meant making weapons instead of automobiles, African Americans helped build aircraft at the Ford Motor Company's Willow Run plant. They also signed on at aircraft plants up and down the West Coast and in industrial states such as Ohio, where the production of shells, tools, Jeeps, and more were helping the war effort. Though they were indeed the last to be hired—and would be the first to be fired at war's end—many blacks were able to purchase decent housing and lead middle-class lives.

The military was a thorny problem for blacks. All United States forces would remain segregated until several years after the end of the war. African-American men were put in all-black units that were supervised by white officers. Though there was resentment, several African-American units distinguished themselves in battle, particularly in Italy and Germany. There were real efforts to keep black men out of the U.S. Navy and the Army Air Corps (later called the Air Force). However, a few African-American pilots were trained at a remote field near Tuskegee, Alabama, and ended up shooting down several enemy planes.

The black press, such as the *Pittsburgh Courier* and other leading newspapers, kept readers informed of the exploits of African Americans. So Robeson had a good idea of what was going on in the military and on the home front. Despite being middle-aged, the singer-actor kept up a fast pace all during the war years. He served as chair of an anticolonial group known as the Council on African Affairs, he spoke and gave concerts across the country, and he starred once again as the tragic hero of the Shakespeare play *Othello*.

Performed on the road in 1942, then opening in New York City in 1943, *Othello* was a stunning success. The actors got along so well that when the director wanted to replace two players, Robeson threatened to quit the production.

Meanwhile, people continued to flock to the performances. Because he was busy and because no actor is great every night, Robeson occasionally let audiences down. "Robeson was rotten," wrote C. L. R. James, the playwright who had written *Toussaint L'Ouverture* a few years earlier.[2] James saw *Othello* in 1944 and caught Robeson standing in one spot, merely saying his lines rather than delivering them with any feeling. The playwright, who was a great fan of

Robeson performs the title role in Shakespeare's *Othello* in 1943, with actress Uta Hagen as Desdemona.

Shakespeare, left the performance deeply disappointed. Robeson seldom faced so harsh a critic.

Nevertheless, Paul Robeson was at the very height of his popularity during the war. He campaigned successfully for the reelection of President Roosevelt in 1944, he worked with major-league baseball so that black players would soon be accepted, and he was joined by twelve thousand people at a party in celebration of his forty-sixth birthday. *Othello* went on the road again after its run in New York City, giving Americans everywhere an opportunity to see classic theater. However, the play was canceled in Indianapolis after the manager could not secure a hotel room for Robeson because of his skin color.

Essie was active on her own during this period. Her projects included getting Paul Jr. off to college, earning a Ph.D. degree in anthropology, and writing a successful book, *African Journey*, about travel in Africa. She was quite remarkable in her own right and was being cited in 1945 by the National Council of Negro Women as one of the country's dozen most outstanding black women.

About the same time, Robeson was given an honorary degree by Howard University, and the National Association for the Advancement of Colored People (NAACP) nominated him for its highest honor, the Spingarn Medal. The Biltmore Hotel in New York City was chosen for the NAACP awards banquet in the fall of 1945, a few months after the war ended. Part of the reason for giving the medal, of course, was for the NAACP to receive favorable publicity. The organization had from its beginning been a voice of reason, seeking full integration by peaceful and lawful means and generally avoiding controversy. Robeson was chosen for the medal in part because he was so widely known and accepted among the white majority. His acceptance speech, however, was anything but mild.

Lingering U.S. fear of the Soviet Union was as much a form of fascism as the Nazi movement in Germany, Robeson told the audience. It was clear to listeners that the entertainer had not been optimistic since the death of President Roosevelt six months earlier. Nor did he take comfort in the formation of the United Nations, as long as the United States made no strong stand on behalf of colonial people worldwide.[3] As his controversial words rang through the ballroom, NAACP members squirmed in their seats. This was not the kind of publicity they had in mind. Robeson "urged the creation of a world where people, whether white, black, red or brown, can live in harmony," the *Pittsburgh Courier* reported.[4]

Today, the speech seems quite reasonable, but at that time the words were highly controversial. The United States felt unusually good about itself in 1945. It was the only remaining superpower. All of the other major countries had either been defeated in World

War II or had been fighting for so long that their economies were in ruins. Millions of people died in the six years of war. Very few of them were American civilians, and war only brushed the United States mainland.

Robeson knew that he was an exception in a country where African Americans were still shut out of the mainstream of life. When black veterans returned home, those considered too confident were chased and beaten. Robeson—and thousands of other African Americans—wondered why blacks should have fought for democracy in Europe when it was not practiced at home. Groups like the NAACP distanced themselves from Robeson's American Crusade to End Lynching, a campaign against those who would be violent toward blacks. The singer-actor pressed for federal help, meeting with President Harry S. Truman in the fall of 1946. The meeting did not go well.

The focus of the American Crusade, as far as Robeson and his friends were concerned, was to press for federal legislation to outlaw lynching. Truman said he most certainly was against lynch mobs but that the time was not right for such lawmaking. When Robeson pointed out that foreign powers might have to intervene if the federal government refused, Truman declared the meeting over.[5] Robeson and Truman were on the same side when it came to lynchings, but the president was feeling political pressure from conservatives, such as FBI director J. Edgar Hoover.

After World War II, Robeson increased his political activism. He knew that he was an exception in a country where African Americans were still shut out of the mainstream of life, and he spoke out passionately for social change.

In the fall of 1946, Robeson was interviewed by the Joint Fact-Finding Committee on Un-American Activities, a California committee chaired by state senator Tenney. The entertainer was a marvelous witness, sparring good-naturedly with his questioners. Ever the teacher, Robeson pointed out that the first people to die at the hands of the Nazis had been Communists and that black people continued to suffer discrimination in this country. He denied being a Communist. Most participants left the hearings smiling.

Meanwhile, Robeson was a financially successful man with a troubled personal life. His marriage had been shaky for many years. He and Essie hardly saw each other; Robeson gave her money through a business agent on a regular basis. Essie often confided in Paul Jr. about money shortages and other family matters. Paul Jr. told her that she and his father were smart enough to work things out. Essie Robeson agreed.[6]

One matter on which the Robesons were in complete agreement was politics. Both were staunch supporters of Henry Wallace, the Progressive Party candidate for president in 1948. He alone among major candidates talked openly of trying to end discrimination against African Americans, of ensuring that they be allowed to vote, attend public school, and so forth. Progressive campaigners went to the heartland and found large numbers of people surprisingly receptive to their speeches. The Democratic Party was nervous about the Progressives and helped interfere with their success.

Throughout the campaign, Progressives were dogged by what seemed to be bad luck. An FBI roundup of U.S. Communist Party members was in the headlines just a few months before the November 1948 vote. Some people associated the Communists with the Progressives. Henry Wallace's popularity and the popularity of his cause started to slide. On election day, only a few more than one million Americans cast their votes for Wallace.

8

THE UNDERDOG

merican public opinion turned against Paul Robeson within a few short years: At the end of 1948 he was respected, sometimes idolized. By 1950 he was the object of scorn, even among a number of African Americans. Ironically, much of the wrath stemmed from a speech Robeson gave—one that was later misquoted. Few Americans took the time or trouble to find what the entertainer had really said while addressing a peace meeting in Paris in the spring of 1949.

Robeson had been politically active all along, traveling to Washington, D.C., before heading for Europe. In the nation's capital he continued to press for laws that would outlaw the lynching of black people. He also wanted to do something about Jim Crow laws, which enforced segregation. These laws prevented African Americans from staying in "whites-only" hotels and from eating in "white" restaurants, for example, in most parts of the United States. Robeson persistently accused politicians of doing nothing, and they in return hinted that he was a Communist.

The trip to Paris was made possible because of an ambitious European concert tour that was planned after a United States tour of eighty-five concerts had been canceled. The American shows were called off after pressure was put on local booking agents not to find times or places for Robeson to sing. The pressure came from the federal government, which was hunting for Communist Party members in the entertainment industry. No one wanted his or her loyalty questioned by Congress simply because he or she had helped Robeson rent an auditorium. So the singer-actor, with his faithful accompanist Larry Brown, departed the country.

Once he landed in Europe, an odd feeling came over Robeson. Despite the problems he faced in the United States, he became homesick.[1] He longed to be back in America, visiting friends, singing, and acting. Most of all, he wanted to speak on behalf of the millions of African Americans without a voice. He certainly was not blind to the country's faults, and he expressed his feelings about them in the speech he gave in Paris before the World Partisans of Peace Congress. Representatives included everyone from Pablo Picasso, the famed artist, to Frederic Joliot-Curie, the son-in-law of renowned scientist Marie Curie.

Specifically, the entertainer called for wealthy Americans to share their money more fairly with the black and white workers who had built the country. Further, he insisted that the average American did not want a war with the Soviets or anyone else. He also was quoted as saying that African Americans would never take up arms against the Soviet Union. An Associated Press reporter incorrectly quoted Robeson as comparing the policies of the United States to those of Nazi Germany.[2] There was an outcry of disapproval in the United States.

Robeson's urge to remain an activist was softened somewhat when he returned home. In the summer of 1949, his son, who had recently earned a degree in engineering, was married to a young white classmate from Cornell University. Though the ceremony was held privately in an apartment, reporters swarmed around outside. Making matters worse, all the white press and many African-American newspapers took this opportunity to condemn the elder Robeson and his political views.

About this time Robeson was involved in the

controversial concert outside Peekskill, New York. Besides the injuries suffered to supporters and the threats to Robeson's safety, the violence indicated that many Americans believed completely what their government said and approved of what it did. The FBI continued to shadow not only Paul but Essie as well.

In 1950, the State Department attempted to quiet Robeson by canceling his passport. The idea was that the Truman administration did not want United States citizens participating in anti-American activities abroad. For Robeson, it meant primarily that he could no longer leave the country. It meant other things to him as well. "What concerns me here is the question of the right to travel in relation to the subject of Negro rights," he wrote, and "there are facts—indisputable facts—which indicate that my concern for Negro rights is indeed at the heart of the case in which I am involved."[3]

Robeson hired attorneys and attempted to get his passport returned. Because his actions were seen as being against the best interests of the United States, the passport stayed in government hands. There was an outcry, but not from the American press. Instead, Communist and non-Communist Europeans condemned the cutting off of the singer-actor's liberties. While Robeson's picture was being removed from a traveling United States exhibit of famous black Americans, he received tributes from abroad. Yet he could not respond in person to the good feeling in

When Robeson's political views angered United States government officials, they canceled his passport so he could no longer travel outside the United States.

Europe because he was not permitted to cross the Atlantic Ocean.

Pressure was also being applied on moderate black leaders by federal authorities. The easiest way to prove loyalty to the United States was to denounce someone considered radical. "Sugar Ray" Robinson, an immensely popular professional boxer, was one of many African Americans to condemn Robeson for his stands on the issues. The black press chimed in, accusing the entertainer of many things that were at best exaggerated and at worst simply untrue. One newspaper printed a list of past recipients of the NAACP Spingarn Medal and left Robeson's name off the list.

Paul Robeson split African-American feelings down the middle. Most African-American politicians, such as Congressman Adam Clayton Powell, Jr., attacked the entertainer with glee. Members of the NAACP wrote critical newspaper editorials, sometimes hiding their identities by not signing the pieces. In contrast, numerous African-American veterans endorsed the notion that they had wasted their time fighting for democracy abroad when it did not exist for them at home.

Besides keeping him out of the headlines, the United States government was depriving Robeson of the means to earn a living. Fortunately, he had saved enough money so he could travel the country, making new friends. Among them was W. E. B. Du Bois, a famous African-American scholar who, like Robeson, had for many years spoken out on behalf of fellow African Americans. Thirty years older than Robeson, Du Bois had received a Ph.D. from Harvard University in 1895. He used his education to dedicate himself to a lifetime of activism. Like Robeson, he saw politics as a means of gaining racial equality.

Still, not everyone was cheated out of hearing Paul Robeson. He gave smaller concerts in less expensive theaters, so more and more African Americans had the opportunity to hear him for the first time. Previously, they had not always been able to afford a downtown concert, nor were they always welcome. But Robeson's income from an average singing engagement slid from $6,000 to $300, and the $300 was made up in part from tickets costing $5 or less. Though he was fading from the entertainment pages of major daily newspapers, the singer was making himself available to a whole new set of fans.

While attorneys fought over his passport, Robeson wrote a column for a small magazine he helped found called *Freedom*. In February 1951, the singer-actor's modest monthly essay was overshadowed by an article critical of him in *Ebony*, a leading black magazine. The article was especially hurtful because it was written by an African American. The writer said Robeson was supportive of the Soviet Union but that he did not

Robeson became friends with W. E. B. Du Bois, the famous African-American scholar and activist.

attempt to help correct the flaws in his own country.[4] Essie Robeson wrote a stinging rebuttal to the piece, but *Ebony* refused to publish it.

In the spring of that year, a judge again dismissed Robeson's appeal for the return of his passport, but the entertainer was buoyed by the birth of his first grand-child. He stayed busy that summer with, among other things, a huge peace rally in Chicago. Following his appearance, Robeson was approached in a hotel lobby by the legendary jazz musician Charlie Parker. "I just wanted to shake your hand," Parker said. "You're a great man."[5]

Because of the controversial positions he took on the issues, Robeson's income decreased considerably. More concerned with civil rights than with a fat bank account, Robeson tried to turn some money over to *Freedom*, the struggling little political-literary magazine he helped start. But his business manager stepped in, pointing out that he could no longer afford to be so generous.

At the time, coincidences in world affairs proved to be important. The Soviet Union awarded Robeson one of its International Stalin Peace Prizes in 1952 at almost the exact time that the U.S. State Department was deciding once again whether to return the enter-tainer's passport. The American government wanted to see a change in attitude, but Robeson's views on civil rights, peace, and freedom were as strong as ever. The singer-actor continued to feel that the right to a passport should not hinge on a person's politics. The State Department turned him down.

Normally, a passport was not required to enter Canada or Mexico. But Robeson was stopped while attempting to visit Canada in 1952, which prevented him from giving a concert. Or did it? The concert was to benefit a Canadian labor union, so the union members came to the U.S.-Canadian border. Robeson serenaded the workers by standing on United States soil and singing to them across the international boundary.

Joseph Stalin, the Soviet dictator, died in 1953. Hints out of Moscow indicated that relations between the Soviet Union and the United States could improve. A few months later, in the summer of 1953, the three-year-old Korean conflict ended. Around the same time, Julius and Ethel Rosenberg were sentenced to be electrocuted in Upstate New York. The two Jewish Americans had been found guilty of selling nuclear secrets to the Soviets. Robeson, always sympathetic to Jews, spoke at rallies held in a vain attempt to prevent the deaths of the couple.

A second Robeson grandchild came along in 1953. Paul Jr., his wife, and their two young children found life to be a struggle. Though Paul Jr. never said much about it to his father, he suffered for the elder Robeson's political activism. Although he was an engineer, Paul Jr. had a tough time finding work, and being black did not help. He landed a job with a physics lab on Long Island, outside New York City, but the FBI warned the lab not to keep him as an employee, and he was quickly let go. Paul Jr. managed a meager living by teaching part-time and writing technical material.

The Robeson family home in Enfield, Connecticut, was put on the market. It was too big for Essie Robeson, who usually was the only one there. Paul Robeson had by 1953 quit coming to Connecticut. Instead, he stayed with friends in New York City, which served all his adult life as the hub of his activity. Once the Enfield home was sold, Essie moved into a suite of rooms in a New York City hotel.

In the summer of 1953, Essie Robeson was summoned to appear before a U.S. Senate investigating committee to explain various passages in her 1945 book, *African Journey*. In it, she had made several remarks that some interpreted as anti-American. Senator Joseph McCarthy, who had been looking for Communists everywhere for several years, wanted to get at Essie Robeson's husband by confronting her.

Essie told the senators that she was proud to be Paul Robeson's wife, that whether she was a Communist or not was, constitutionally, none of their business, and she emphasized the fact that she and all other African Americans were treated like second-class citizens. She said she knew no one who wanted to overthrow the federal government, and she forced McCarthy and his fellow senators to define and choose their words carefully. Luckily, Essie Robeson was not cited for contempt for standing up for her family and for her race.[6]

9

IN DECLINE

The years of being spied upon, bugged, misquoted, and harassed were taking their toll on Paul Robeson. One day in 1955, the usually healthy singer-actor noticed traces of blood in his urine. Robeson had been in a hospital only once in his life—for the leg injury he suffered while playing football. He consulted a doctor about this new ailment, and the doctor recommended surgery. Robeson suspected a plot by the FBI to get him into the hospital, but he did agree to the surgery.[1]

The operation did not go well. Robeson was in the hospital a total of three weeks. He was released and moved in with Essie in a Harlem apartment. Friends were surprised to learn that the two were living together again. Both were ill and each needed the support of the other. Essie had survived a difficult operation for cancer, then returned to being as active as ever. This activity helped conceal the fact that she was still dying of the disease.

Robeson recovered slowly. Not until the end of 1955 did he give a concert, this one in Ontario. He was permitted to leave and reenter the United States, but only under circumstances where no passport was required. So he sang where it was important, this time to the loyal miners and millwrights in the Canadian union that had supported him through the years. The concert for the union members was followed by a larger event in Toronto before the singer returned to New York City.

Robeson's health worsened. He was diagnosed as manic-depressive, a mental condition that is now called bipolar disorder. Typically, manic-depressives are either very happy or extremely unhappy, with no in-between moods. When Robeson felt good, he spent hour after hour devouring information. For example, he became fascinated with musical theory.

Prescription drugs failed to alleviate Robeson's physical and mental symptoms. By the spring of 1956, he was in a downward spiral of depression. Several doctors debated what to do as the entertainer refused any psychiatric help. About the same time, the congressional House Un-American Activities Committee (HUAC) ordered him to come to Washington for more grilling about his connection with communism. Despite letters from several doctors telling of his ill health, HUAC granted Robeson a rest of only two weeks. With family and friends, he headed for the nation's capitol.

Entering the hearing room, Robeson had a glazed look. Friends and loved ones feared the congressmen would pick him apart, tearing into a man whose mind was not what it once had been. In fact Robeson traded sharp remarks with his adversaries, replying to their questions with questions of his own. He finally pleaded the Fifth Amendment to the Constitution, which states that an American does not have to answer questions that would tend to incriminate him.[2]

When the House committee members and their lawyers failed to learn whether Robeson was a Communist, they asked him why he had not stayed in the Soviet Union when he had the opportunity. Robeson replied that he returned to help free his fellow African Americans, to battle fascism, and to make things like equal housing and equal education a reality for everyone. Congressmen reminded Robeson that Communist prisons were full of dissenters; Robeson told them that there were many African Americans treated unfairly by the United States criminal justice system.[3] Surprisingly, his reactions to this harsh

In the 1950s, the United States government was questioning anyone who they believed was sympathetic to the Communists. Both Paul and Essie (above) Robeson were called to testify before the Senate investigating committee.

treatment in Washington made Robeson seem like his old self.

Nevertheless, he was not the African American who was making the headlines. Rather, it was a modest woman named Rosa Parks. The Montgomery, Alabama, seamstress refused on December 1, 1955, to give her seat to a white man on a public bus in her hometown. Her refusal led to the boycott of the bus system by blacks and to the rise of Martin Luther King, Jr., to lead the civil rights movement. King had studied the nonviolent resistance of Mohandas Gandhi of India and applied it successfully in an effort to desegregate the American South. Robeson played no direct part in the movement.

Finally, in the spring of 1957, the government consented to talk about the status of Robeson's passport. He and Essie went to Washington once again. If the Robesons were less apprehensive, they were also less successful than the last time they had made the journey. Once again the bureaucrats asked Robeson about his Communist Party connection, and once again the entertainer refused to say anything. The hearing ended when Robeson would not sign an anti-Communist statement. Later that same year, he received permission to travel throughout the Western Hemisphere.

Meanwhile, English friends were rallying to Robeson's support. Several roles were offered to

Robeson for the 1958 London play season, but without a passport he could not make any promises. His public statements became less controversial. For the time being, Robeson's deep bass voice made a lasting impression in concert more than anywhere else.

In 1958, *Here I Stand* was published. Robeson's combination of autobiography and philosophy was snubbed by the white media and largely praised by black publications. But it was widely read and favorably reviewed everywhere from India to Japan to Great Britain. Rather than reciting dates and places, the book was a call to action. "The time is now," Robeson wrote, for African Americans to claim the rights granted to the United States majority.[4] The call for equality came several years before the freedom rides and sit-ins that were signatures of the civil rights movement in the 1960s.

Equally important, Robeson spent some time at a recording studio and made several memorable recordings for the respected Vanguard label. He also celebrated his sixtieth birthday and, for the first time in more than a decade, performed in New York City. The site was Carnegie Hall, and tickets sold out quickly to fans eager to hear the singer reunite with his longtime accompanist, Larry Brown.

Even more significant, after eight years of confrontation, Robeson was given back his passport. The State Department handed back the document as a result of a U.S. Supreme Court ruling in another passport-related matter. The entertainer immediately announced that he was heading for Europe to perform, not as an activist but as an artist. The reception he received in England, where he had always been extremely popular, was very warm. Hundreds of fans and friends met him at the airport in London.

Following a television appearance and other public appearances, Paul and Essie Robeson flew to Moscow for a series of concerts throughout the Soviet Union. The welcome was tumultuous, but the heat and the crowds affected the singer. He came down with a fever and spent several days in bed. After he recovered, Robeson returned to England for additional performances, promising to go back to the Soviet Union soon. He did so at the end of 1958. This time, Robeson fell ill shortly after attending a state dinner that included Soviet Premier Nikita Khrushchev. The entertainer felt dizzy and was hospitalized.

As it turned out, both of the Robesons needed medical treatment. Essie's cancer was acting up, and her husband was found by doctors to be completely exhausted. Robeson slowly regained his strength, enough so that by the spring of 1959 he left Moscow for London—leaving Essie behind for additional treatment. Robeson was committed to star in *Othello* once again, and he gave a sound performance. Later that

Robeson was called upon to star as *Othello* many times throughout his life.

year, Essie and Paul Jr. and family joined Robeson in London. Things seemed to be looking up.

After *Othello* closed, the Robesons visited several European countries. People who had known the entertainer for a long time noted that he had aged greatly. They also witnessed mood swings—he was happy and upbeat one minute and deeply depressed the next. Essie was not well, and Paul was homesick. He went on a crash diet that caused him to lose forty pounds in forty days. Essie found him more difficult to get along with. The Robesons toured Australia and New Zealand, only to return to London and have the singer-actor complain that he had nothing to do.

With little notice to anyone, Robeson flew to Moscow in the late winter of 1961. On arrival, he spoke with Essie by phone and seemed to be in good spirits. But shortly afterward, the sixty-two-year-old attempted suicide by slashing his wrists.

10

LIFE'S TWILIGHT

aul Jr., who could always be relied on, flew to Moscow to find out about his father's condition. Robeson had slit his wrists in the early hours of the morning. He had done it in his hotel suite bath with adoring fans in nearby rooms. No one was sure how much blood he had lost or exactly when the attempt had occurred.

Soviet doctors said he was suffering from a mental disease related to atherosclerosis, or hardening of the arteries. Despite her own ills, Essie flew to Moscow. It was her job to stifle rumors, and she held off the often hostile press very well.[1] Several weeks later, in June of 1962, all three Robesons returned to London. Paul joined Larry Brown, and the two worked at times on their music. Doctors continued Robeson's treatment in England, where his moods swung from one extreme to the other. In the English hospital in which he was a frequent patient, doctors began to give him electric shock treatments. They believed that he was chronically depressed and that powerful jolts of electricity to his troubled brain could permanently improve his outlook. Paul Jr. was angry that his mother allowed such treatment. He would later say that the shock treatments permanently damaged his father's brain.[2]

Robeson was given dozens of electric shock treatments. Between his visits to the hospital, he had delusions about how people or governments were out to get him. At times, the shock therapy brought improvement. Famed African-American vocalist Ella Fitzgerald gave a London concert and the Robesons attended. Fitzgerald was told that Robeson was in the audience and said some kind things about him. Afterward, he met her in her dressing room and the two chatted warmly. Robeson also attended Chekov's play *The Cherry Orchard*, which featured his old friend Peggy Ashcroft, who had been his co-star decades earlier in *Othello*. He went backstage there, too, and the two theater veterans promised each other they would give a public poetry reading together in the near future.

About the same time, the Robesons had to renew

their passports. They obeyed all the rules, dropping the documents at the U.S. Embassy in London. But time passed and they heard nothing. They went to the embassy in person and learned that the State Department wanted them to swear that they were not Communists. Essie did so immediately. Paul had never signed such a statement and was not about to do so now. Essie and his friends convinced him that the pledge was unimportant, or at least of less importance than a fresh passport. He finally signed and the new passports were issued promptly. The couple returned to the United States.

Years later, Robeson's granddaughter wrote:

> At the airport in New York, the press was out in full force, poised for attack. But my family and a few close friends were there, and as Paul and Essie stepped off the plane we immediately surrounded them, partly to protect them from the onslaught of the press, whose members pressed around, cameras snapping, popping off all manner of hostile questions. The next day, true to form, the headline in *The New York Times* appeared: "Paul Robeson: Disillusioned Native Son." It didn't matter what my grandfather said or did; the press had a picture they wanted to paint.[3]

Robeson spent much of this time trying to recover his physical and mental health, a task made more difficult because Essie's condition was deteriorating. They traveled to California for a "Salute to Paul Robeson" event, but at the last minute the star of the show felt too tired to attend. Robeson slid into depression once more.

Both Robesons continued to battle ill health. Essie became so sick with the symptoms of cancer that Paul moved to Philadelphia, where his sister Marian Robeson Forsythe, a retired teacher, could look after him. He suffered through several illnesses, including pneumonia. Meanwhile, Essie was receiving powerful cobalt treatments in a New York City hospital. After the ailing Robesons returned to their Harlem apartment, Essie was confined to bed.

She was readmitted to the hospital in November 1965. Fighting to breathe, she had become mute but still welcomed visitors. She died on December 13, 1965, two days before her seventieth birthday. Robeson was at his sister's Philadelphia home when Paul Jr. broke the news to him. Continuing to suffer from mental and physical illnesses, he silently signed his wife's death certificate. Paul Jr. and his wife and children attended Essie's funeral without Paul Robeson.

Much of the last decade of Robeson's life was spent with his sister in her comfortable Philadelphia home. The entertainer had a number of visitors, but family members noted that his strength was fading, and they cooperated in making his last few years quiet ones.[4]

Paul Robeson, who had been beloved around the world, and then persecuted by the United States

This bust of Paul Robeson was created by Russian sculptor Bernice Marker for the Moorland-Spingarn Research Center at Howard University in Washington, D.C.

government and scorned by many, began to regain his public stature. In 1969, Rutgers University dedicated a music and arts lounge to Paul Robeson. A few years later, the school gave a presentation on his life. Administrators at the college knew that the alumnus from long ago had forged a trail for so many of their black graduates. Other honors arrived, from as near as the National Association for the Advancement of Colored People (NAACP) in New York City to as far away as the German Democratic Republic.

In 1973, a multimedia salute to Paul Robeson on his seventy-fifth birthday packed Carnegie Hall in New York City. Robeson did not attend, but he sent a recorded message, which said, in part: "I want you to know I am the same Paul, dedicated as ever to the worldwide cause of humanity for freedom, peace, and brotherhood. My heart is with the continuing struggle of my own people. . . ."[5]

In December 1975, three days before New Year's Eve, Robeson was hospitalized after a mild stroke. He grew weaker and weaker, suffered at least one more stroke, and died in his sleep on January 23, 1976. Funeral ceremonies were held in his brother Ben's Harlem church, where the crowd of black and white friends and admirers overflowed onto the wintry sidewalk.

11

PAUL ROBESON'S
LEGACY

he late historian and civil rights advocate
W. E. B. Du Bois summed up the controversy
surrounding the political life of Paul
Robeson:

> It was that while he did not rail at America he did
> praise the Soviet Union, and he did that because it
> treated him like a man and not a dog. . . . The children
> of Russia clung to him; the workers greeted him; the
> state named mountains after him. . . . Never before
> had he received such treatment. . . . In America he was
> a "niggar"; in Britain he was tolerated; in France he
> was cheered; in the Soviet Union he was loved for the
> great artist that he is.[1]

But Paul Robeson's controversial activism could never
eclipse his astounding range of talents. His singing voice

was so remarkable that it almost seemed to have a life of its own. Robeson stood out in sports as well as in show business long before the two became as intertwined as they are now. At the same time, there was a widespread effort to silence him by those in government—even though he had broken no laws. Still, Robeson refused to give up and was able for years to look clearly into the future and explain what life should ideally be like for African Americans.

At times, it seemed as though with each new success in Paul Robeson's life came yet another obstacle that had to be overcome. Despite his singing, his acting, his intellectual and athletic talents, Robeson was still ruled by the laws of segregation.

He was prohibited from using the same public accommodations that his audiences used without a second thought. Concerts were canceled because there was no place for Robeson to stay, even in major cities. When government officials accused Robeson of being a Communist, he was further prevented from performing.

Although Robeson won great fame overseas, his passport was taken away from him, and he was barred from leaving the United States and performing for the very people who seemed to appreciate him most. Despite breaking through many barriers both onstage and on the playing field, it was not until 1995, nineteen years after his death, that Paul Robeson was inducted into the College Football Hall of Fame. No other All-American player ever met that kind of delay.

With such a mixed outlook, did Paul Robeson's activism do anyone any good?

The answer is yes. Every black and Latino player in major-league baseball owes Robeson a debt because he clamored for the admission of minorities into the big leagues several years before Jackie Robinson put on a Brooklyn Dodger uniform in 1947. Meaningful screen roles are now routinely given to black actors. Prime-time television features a number of blacks and other minorities onscreen as well as in the director's chair and in the production office. At last, African Americans are portrayed with the same complexity and depth of character as the rest of the population.

Robeson showed African Americans, many of whom had never seen a black man in a coat and tie, that they could compete in any area. Robeson's academic accomplishments demonstrated that a solid education is one way to leave poverty behind. Perhaps most important for every American, Paul Robeson showed real courage in standing up for ideas that the black and white establishments found frightening. That he suffered greatly underscores his dedication to his beliefs.

With an eye on his songs, movies, sports, and stage performances, Paul Robeson took center stage again in 1998, the centennial of his birth. Committees all around the United States organized special exhibits and tributes to honor the memory of this remarkable actor, singer, athlete, and political activist. On February 25, 1998, twenty-two years after his death, Paul Robeson was awarded a Grammy Award for lifetime achievement in music.

Harry Belafonte, another famous African-American singer and activist, spoke fondly of Robeson in the spring of 1997. He took part in a salute to American veterans of the Spanish civil war—the conflict where Robeson calmed a battlefield with his melodious voice as soldiers on both sides laid down their weapons to listen. Belafonte noted to great applause that he himself had signed on to fight in World War II as a teenager after being inspired by Paul Robeson.

Belafonte learned from Robeson that artistic talent could be used to help make the world a better place, that "the purpose of art is not just to show life as it is, but to show life as it should be." "Harry," Robeson once told him, "get them to sing your song, and they will want to know who you are." When this type of sharing occurs, a step has been taken toward a greater understanding between people.[2]

Belafonte had visited Paul Robeson in 1976, during the final days of Robeson's life. Had Robeson's often painful struggle against inequality and injustice been worth it, Belafonte wondered: "Paul . . . considering the platform you had gained, and how easy life could have been for you, was it worth it?" Robeson responded: "Harry, make no mistake; there is no aspect of what I have done that wasn't worth it. . . . Beyond the victory itself, infinitely more important, was the journey."[3]

In 1937, on a radio broadcast for a rally in support of the antifascist forces fighting in the Spanish civil war, Paul Robeson spoke the words that sum up his life and his beliefs. These words are inscribed on his tombstone: "The artist must elect to fight for freedom or for slavery. I have made my choice. I had no alternative."[4]

CHRONOLOGY

1898—Paul Leroy Robeson is born on April 9 in Princeton, New Jersey.

1904—Mother dies of burns in accidental home fire; father raises family of five children.

1915—Graduates with honors from Somerville, New Jersey, high school; enters Rutgers College, where he successfully tries out for varsity football.

1918—Father dies at the age of seventy-three.

1919—During his four years at Rutgers, Paul wins fifteen varsity letters in four different sports—football, basketball, baseball, and track; graduates from college as valedictorian of his class.

1920—Enters Columbia University Law School.

1921—Marries Eslanda ("Essie") Cardozo Goode.

1923—Graduates from law school.

1924—Plays the lead in two Eugene O'Neill plays, *All God's Chillun Got Wings* and a revival of *The Emperor Jones*; agrees to star in the silent movie *Body and Soul*.

1925—Gives first concert with piano accompanist Laurence Brown; stars in *The Emperor Jones* in London; records Negro spirituals for Victor Records.

1926—Begins first United States tour; plays the lead in *Black Boy*, a play about boxing.

1927—Son, Paul Jr., is born in New York.

1928—Opens in *Show Boat* in London.

1930—Plays the title role in *Othello* in London.

1933—Stars in movie version of *The Emperor Jones*.

1934—Travels to the Soviet Union to discuss film projects.

1935—Stars in film version of *Show Boat*.

1936—Enrolls nine-year-old Paul Jr. in a Moscow public school.

1938—Travels to Spain.

1939—Stars in mining film, *Proud Valley*.

1941—Buys home in rural Connecticut; sings and speaks at a rally for Earl Browder, imprisoned head of the American Communist Party.

1942—Gives time and talent to concerts in support of the war effort.

1943—Appears in *Othello* on Broadway to great critical acclaim.

1945—Awarded Spingarn Medal, highest honor given each year by the National Association for the Advancement of Colored People (NAACP).

1946—Joins in sponsoring a crusade against lynching, meeting unsuccessfully with President Harry S. Truman in an effort to get the president's support.

1948—Campaigns for Progressive Party presidential candidate Henry A. Wallace.

1949—Performs in Europe and the Soviet Union; riots take place in Peekskill, New York, in connection with a Robeson concert.

1950—U.S. State Department revokes Robeson's passport.

1952—Awarded Soviet Union's International Stalin Peace Prize.

1953—Sells home in Connecticut.

1956—Appears before congressional House Un-American Activities Committee (HUAC).

1958—Wins back his passport; leaves quickly for Great Britain and European and Soviet concert tour; book *Here I Stand* is published.

1963—Returns to New York City.

1965—Essie Robeson dies of cancer at age sixty-nine.

1969—Rutgers University names music and arts lounge after Robeson.

1973—Salute to Paul Robeson on his seventy-fifth birthday packs New York's Carnegie Hall.

1976—Dies on January 23 at the age of seventy-seven in a Philadelphia hospital.

1998—Centennial celebration pays tribute to Paul Robeson with special exhibits and events throughout the United States.

PAUL ROBESON PERFORMS

Selected Discography

Ballad for Americans (Vanguard, 1990)
Collectors Paul Robeson (Monitor, 1993)
The Essential Paul Robeson (Vanguard, 1987)
Green Pastures (ASV/Living Era, 1992)
Live at Carnegie Hall—May 9, 1958 (Vanguard, 1987)
A Lonesome Road (ASV/Living Era, 1992)
A Man and His Beliefs—Golden Classics
    Vol. 2 (Collectibles Records, 1991)
Man and His Beliefs (Legacy, 1997)
The Odyssey of Paul Robeson (Vanguard Classics, 1998)
Paul Robeson (Pearl Flapper, 1993)
Paul Robeson Favorite Songs, Vol. 1 (Monitor Records, 1992)
The Peace Arch Concerts (Folk Era, 1997)
The Power and the Glory (Sony Music, 1991)

Filmography

Body and Soul, 1924
Borderline, 1929
Emperor Jones, 1933
Sanders of the River, 1935
Show Boat, 1936
Song of Freedom, 1936
King Solomon's Mines, 1937
Jericho, 1937
Big Fella, 1938
Proud Valley, 1939
Tales of Manhattan, 1942

Chapter Notes

Chapter 1. Violence in Peekskill

1. Susan Robeson, *The Whole World in His Hands* (Secaucus, N.J.: Citadel Press, 1981), p. 180.

2. Philip S. Foner, ed., *Paul Robeson Speaks: Writings, Speeches, Interviews, 1918–1974* (New York: Brunner/Mazel Publishers, 1978), p. 235.

3. Robeson, p. 180.

4. Ibid., p. 186.

Chapter 2. A New Jersey Boyhood

1. Paul Robeson, *Here I Stand* (Boston: Beacon Press, 1958), p. 6.

2. Ibid., p. 7.

3. Robert V. Hoffman, *The Olde Towne Scrapbook* (Westfield, N.J., 1945), p. 82.

4. Robeson, p. 9.

5. Martin Bauml Duberman, *Paul Robeson* (New York: Knopf, 1989), p. 13.

6. Ibid., p. 16.

7. Robeson, p. 25.

Chapter 3. College and Marriage

1. Martin Bauml Duberman, *Paul Robeson* (New York: Knopf, 1989), p. 23.

2. Eslanda Goode Robeson, *Paul Robeson, Negro* (New York: Harper and Brothers, 1930), p. 176.

3. Ibid., p. 177.

4. Paul Robeson, "The New Idealism," *The Targum* (Rutgers University), June 1919, p. 571.

5. Ibid.

6. Philip S. Foner, ed., *Paul Robeson Speaks: Writings, Speeches, Interviews, 1918–1974* (New York: Brunner/Mazel Publishers, 1978), p. 65.

7. Eslanda Goode Robeson, p. 69.

8. Lloyd L. Brown, *The Young Paul Robeson* (Boulder, Colo.: Westview Press, 1997), p. 107.

9. Duberman, p. 37.
10. Ibid., p. 43.
11. Ibid., p. 51.
12. Brown, p. 114.
13. Susan Robeson, *The Whole World in His Hands* (Secaucus, N.J.: Citadel Press, 1981), p. 33.

Chapter 4. Show Business

1. Martin Bauml Duberman, *Paul Robeson* (New York: Knopf, 1989), p. 79.
2. Lloyd L. Brown, *The Young Paul Robeson* (Boulder, Colo.: Westview Press, 1997), p. 123.
3. Paul Robeson, *Here I Stand* (Boston: Beacon Press, 1958), p. 32.
4. Brown, p. 124.

Chapter 5. Africa and the Soviet Union

1. Eslanda Goode Robeson, *Paul Robeson, Negro* (New York: Harper & Brothers, 1930), p. 157.
2. The Editors of Freedomways, *Paul Robeson, the Great Forerunner* (New York: Dodd, Mead and Company, 1977), pp. 51–53.
3. T. Thompson, "Paul Robeson Speaks about Art and the Negro," *The Millgate* (London), December 1930, pp. 157–158.
4. Martin Bauml Duberman, *Paul Robeson* (New York: Knopf, 1989), p. 176.
5. Philip S. Foner, ed., *Paul Robeson Speaks: Writings, Speeches, Interviews, 1918–1974* (New York: Brunner/Mazel Publishers, 1978), p. 213 .
6. Lloyd L. Brown, *The Young Paul Robeson* (Boulder, Colo.: Westview Press, 1997), p. 125.
7. Virginia Hamilton, *Paul Robeson, The Life and Times of a Free Black Man* (New York: Harper & Row Publishers, 1974), p. 62.
8. Foner, pp. 10–11.
9. Susan Robeson, *The Whole World in His Hands* (Secaucus, N.J.: Citadel Press, 1981), p. 92.
10. Paul Robeson, *Here I Stand* (Boston: Beacon Press, 1958), p. 52.
11. Ibid., p. 54.

Chapter 6. Activism

1. Paul Robeson, *Here I Stand* (Boston: Beacon Press, 1958), p. 53.
2. Philip S. Foner, ed., *Paul Robeson Speaks: Writings, Speeches, Interviews, 1918–1974* (New York: Brunner/Mazell Publishers, 1978), p. 125.
3. Martin Bauml Duberman, *Paul Robeson* (New York: Knopf, 1989), p. 221.
4. Virginia Hamilton, *Paul Robeson, The Life and Times of a Free Black Man* (New York: Harper & Row Publishers, 1974), p. 66.
5. Foner, pp. 140–142.
6. Ibid., p. 140.

Chapter 7. Under Scrutiny

1. Martin Bauml Duberman, *Paul Robeson* (New York: Knopf, 1989), p. 254.
2. Scott McLemee, "A Trotskyite in Love," *The New York Times Book Review*, September 8, 1996, p. 12.
3. Philip S. Foner, ed., *Paul Robeson Speaks: Writings, Speeches, Interviews, 1918–1974* (New York: Brunner/Mazel Publishers, 1978), p. 165.
4. Ibid., p. 162.
5. Robert J. Donovan, *Conflict and Crisis, The Presidency of Harry S. Truman, 1945–1948* (New York: W. W. Norton Company), p. 245.
6. Duberman, pp. 313-314.

Chapter 8. The Underdog

1. Martin Bauml Duberman, *Paul Robeson* (New York: Knopf, 1989), p. 339.
2. Philip S. Foner, ed., *Paul Robeson Speaks: Writings, Speeches, Interviews, 1918–1974* (New York: Brunner/Mazel Publishers, 1978), pp. 197–200.
3. Paul Robeson, *Here I Stand* (Boston: Beacon Press, 1958), p. 63.
4. Walter White, "The Strange Case of Paul Robeson," *Ebony*, February 1951.
5. Duberman, p. 397.
6. Duberman, pp. 412–413.

Chapter 9. In Decline

1. Martin Bauml Duberman, *Paul Robeson* (New York: Knopf, 1989), p. 435.

2. Ibid., pp. 439–440.

3. Philip S. Foner, ed., *Paul Robeson Speaks: Writings, Speeches, Interviews, 1918–1974* (New York: Brunner/Mazell, 1978), p. 433.

4. Paul Robeson, *Here I Stand* (Boston, Beacon Press, 1958), p. 74.

Chapter 10. Life's Twilight

1. Susan Robeson, *The Whole World in His Hands* (Secaucus, N.J.: Citadel Press, 1981), p. 219.

2. Martin Bauml Duberman, *Paul Robeson* (New York: Knopf, 1989), p. 503.

3. Robeson, p. 235.

4. Ibid., p. 236.

5. Laurie Johnston, "Robeson at 75, Is Feted in Absentia," *The New York Times*, April 16, 1973.

Chapter 11. Paul Robeson's Legacy

1. W. E. B. Du Bois, "The Real Reason Behind Robeson's Persecution," *National Guardian*, April 7, 1958.

2. Harry Belafonte, transcription of speech at Manhattan Community College, April 27, 1997. Internet site: <http://www.cs.uchicago.edu/cpsr/robeson/belafonte.html>

3. Ibid.

4. Paul Robeson, *Here I Stand* (Boston: Beacon Press, 1958), p. 52.

FURTHER READING

Brown, Lloyd L. *The Young Paul Robeson: On My Journey Now*. Boulder, Colo: Westview Press, 1997.

Duberman, Martin Bauml. *Paul Robeson*. New York: Knopf, 1989.

Ehrlich, Scott. *Paul Robeson: Singer and Actor*. New York: Chelsea House, 1989.

Hamilton, Virginia. *Paul Robeson: The Life and Times of a Free Black Man*. New York: Harper & Row, 1974.

Larsen, Rebecca. *Paul Robeson, Hero Before His Time*. New York, Franklin Watts, 1989.

McKissack, Patricia, and Fredrick McKissack. *Paul Robeson: A Voice to Remember*. Hillside, N.J.: Enslow Publishers, Inc., 1992.

Robeson, Paul. *Here I Stand*. Boston: Beacon Press, 1958.

Robeson, Paul Jr. *Paul Robeson, Jr. Speaks to America*. New Brunswick, N.J.: Rutgers University Press, 1993.

Robeson, Susan. *The Whole World in His Hands: A Pictorial Biography of Paul Robeson*. Secaucus, N.J.: Citadel Press, 1981.

On the Internet

<http://www.us.net.upa/guides/robeson.htm>

<http://www.motownmagic.com/robeson.html>

<http://pobox.com/~robeson/> *or*
<http:/www.cs.uchicago.edu/cpsr/robeson/>

Videotapes

Paul Robeson: *Tribute to an Artist* (Janus Films, 1979)

Paul Robeson: *The Tallest Tree in Our Forest* (produced by Gil Nobel, 1977)

INDEX

The New York Tribune, 24
New York University, 28, 29

O

O'Neill, Eugene, 37, 40
Othello, 17, 51–52, 77, 103, 105,
107
L'Ouverture, Toussaint, 19

P

Parker, Charlie, 57, 93
Parks, Rosa, 101
Paul Robeson, Negro, 49, 51
Pittsburgh Courier, 77, 80
Plant in the Sun, 67
Powell, Adam Clayton, Jr., 90
Presbyterian church, 12
Princeton University, 19
The Proud Valley, 70–71
Provincetown Players, 37, 38
Pulitzer Prize, 47

R

Robeson, Benjamin, 12, 13, 18
Robeson, Eslanda Cardozo Goode
(Essie), 30, 32–33, 34, 36, 44,
45, 47, 48, 49, 53, 54, 60, 64,
70, 72, 79, 83, 88, 95–96,
97–98, 101, 103, 105, 106,
107–109
Robeson, John, 12
Robeson, Maria Louisa Bustill, 11,
13
Robeson, Marian, 12, 13, 109
Robeson, Paul
academic honors, 26
birth of, 11
communism, 5–6, 7, 9, 10, 55,
58, 62, 65, 71, 72, 75,
80–81, 83, 93–94, 99, 108
death of, 111

marriage, 33
Peeksill confrontation, 5–10, 88
singing voice, 6, 8, 18, 41, 42,
Robeson, Paul Jr., 47, 53–54, 60,
87, 94, 106, 107, 109
Robeson, William Drew, 11–16,
17, 18, 25, 26
Robeson, William Jr., 12
Robinson, Jackie, 114
Robinson, "Sugar Ray," 90
Roosevelt, Eleanor, 75
Roosevelt, Franklin D., 72–73, 75,
79
Roseanne, 40
Rosenberg, Julius and Ethel, 94
Rutgers University, 20, 21, 23, 24,
25–26, 28, 30, 54, 110

S

Sanford, G. Foster, 23, 29
Scottsboro Boys, 58–59
Show Boat, 48, 49, 54, 59
Shuffle Along, 34
Song of Freedom, 60
Stalin, Joseph, 65, 94

T

Taboo, 34
Toussaint L'Ouverture, 59, 77
Truman, Harry S., 10, 81

V

Vanguard Records, 102
Vanity Fair, 42
Victor Talking Machine Company
(RCA), 42
Voodoo, 34, 36

W

Wallace, Henry, 83, 84